Famous Women.

MARY LAMB.

The next volumes in the Famous Women Series will be:

Already published:

MARY LAMB.

BY

ANNE GILCHRIST.

BOSTON:
ROBERTS BROTHERS.
1884.

UNIVERSITY PRESS:
JOHN WILSON AND SON, CAMBRIDGE.

PREFACE.

I AM indebted to Mrs. Henry Watson, a grand-daughter of Mr. Gillman, for one or two interesting reminiscences, and for a hitherto unpublished "notelet" by Lamb (page 327), together with an omitted paragraph from a published letter (page 110), which confirms what other letters also show, — that the temporary estrangement between Lamb and Coleridge was mainly due to the influence of the morbid condition of mind of their common friend, Charles Lloyd.

My thanks are also due to Mr. Potts for some bibliographic details respecting the various editions of the *Tales from Shakespeare*.

Reprinted here, for the first time, is a little essay on *Needlework* (regarded from an industrial, not an "art" point of view), by Mary Lamb (page 244), unearthed from an obscure and long-deceased periodical — *The British*

Lady's Magazine—for which I have to thank Mr. Edward Solly, F. R. S.

The reader will find, also, the only letter that has been preserved from Coleridge to Lamb, who destroyed all the rest in a moment of depression (pages 32–3). This letter is given, without exact date or name of the person to whom it was addressed, in Gillman's unfinished *Life of Coleridge*, as having been written "to a friend in great anguish of mind on the sudden death of his mother," and has, I believe, never before been identified. But the internal evidence that it was to Lamb is decisive.

In taking Mary as the central figure in the following narrative, woven mainly from her own and her brother's letters and writings, it is to that least explored time, from 1796 to 1815 — before they had made the acquaintance of Judge Talfourd, Procter, Patmore, De Quincey and other friends, who have left written memorials of them—that we are brought nearest ; the period, that is, of Charles' youth and early manhood. For Mary was the elder by ten years ; and there is but little to tell of the last twenty of her eighty-three years of life, when the burthen of age was added to that of her sad malady.

The burial register of St. Andrew's, Holborn, in which churchyard Lamb's father, mother and Aunt Hetty were buried, shows that the father survived his wife's tragic death nearly three years instead of only a few months, as Talfourd and others following him have supposed. It is a date of some interest, because not till then did brother and sister begin together their life of "double singleness" and entire mutual devotion. Also, in sifting the letters for facts and dates, I find that Lamb lived in Chapel street, Pentonville, not, as Talfourd and Procter thought, a few months, but three years, removing thither almost immediately after the mother's death. It is a trifle, yet not without interest to the lovers of Lamb, for these were the years in which he met in his daily walks, and loved but never accosted, the beautiful Quakeress "Hester," whose memory is enshrined in the poem beginning "When maidens such as Hester die."

ANNE GILCHRIST.

Keats Corner, Hampstead.

CONTENTS.

CHAPTER I.

CHAPTER II.

CHAPTER III.

CHAPTER IV.

CHAPTER V.

CHAPTER VI.

CHAPTER VII.

LIST OF AUTHORITIES.

Life, Letters and Writings of Charles Lamb. Edited
by Percy Fitzgerald, M. A., F. S. A. 1876.

The Works of Charles Lamb. Edited by Charles Kent,
(in which, for the first time, the dates and original
mode of publication were affixed to the Essays,
etc.) 1878.

Poetry for Children, by Charles and Mary Lamb.
Edited by Richard Herne Shepherd. 1878.

Mrs. Leicester's School, by Charles and Mary Lamb.

Tales from Shakespeare, by Charles and Mary Lamb.
1807.

Final Memorials of Charles Lamb, by Talfourd. 1848.

Charles Lamb: A Memoir, by Barry Cornwall. 1866.

Mary and Charles Lamb, by W. Carew Hazlitt. 1874.

My Friends and Acquaintance, by P. G. Patmore. 1854.

Letters, Conversations and Recollections of Coleridge,
by Thomas Allsop. Third edition. 1864.

Early Recollections of Coleridge, by J. Cottle. 1837.

Biographia Literaria, by Coleridge. Second edition.
1847.

Life of Coleridge, by Gillman. Vol. I. 1838.

Memoirs and Letters of Sara Coleridge. Edited by her
Daughter. 1873.

Life of Wordsworth, by Rev. Dr. C. Wordsworth.
1851.

A Chronological List of the Writings of Hazlitt and Leigh Hunt, preceded by an Essay on Lamb, and List of his Works, by Alex. Ireland; printed for private circulation. (The copy used contains many MS. additions by the author.)   1868.

Recollections of Writers, by Charles and Mary Cowden-Clarke.   1878.

Six Life Studies of Famous Women, by M. Betham Edwards.   1880.

Diary, Reminiscences and Correspondence of Henry Crabb Robinson. Edited by Dr. Sadler.   1869.

Memoirs of William Hazlitt, by W. Carew Hazlitt. 1867.

Spirit of the Age. } Hazlitt.   1825, 1826.
Table Talk.

Autobiographical Sketches. } De Quincey.   1863.
Lakes and Lake Poets.

William Godwin, his Friends and Contemporaries, by Kegan Paul.   1876.

MARY LAMB.

CHAPTER I.

Parentage and Childhood.

1764–1775. — Æt. 1–10.

THE story of Mary Lamb's life is mainly the story of a brother and sister's love; of how it sustained them under the shock of a terrible calamity, and made beautiful and even happy a life which must else have sunk into desolation and despair.

It is a record, too, of many friendships. Round the biographer of Mary as of Charles, the blended stream of whose lives cannot be divided into two distinct currents, there gathers a throng of faces — radiant, immortal faces some, many homely, every-day faces, a few almost grotesque — whom he can no more shut out of his pages, if he would give a faithful picture of life and character, than Charles or Mary could have shut their humanity-loving hearts or hospitable doors against them. First comes Coleridge, earliest and best-beloved friend of all, to whom Mary was "a most dear heart's sister;" Wordsworth and his sister Dorothy; Southey; Hazlitt, who, quarrel with whom he might, could not effectually quarrel with the Lambs; his wife, also, without whom Mary would have been a comparatively silent figure to us, a presence rather than a voice. But all kinds were welcome so there were but character; the more variety the better. "I am made up of queer points," wrote Lamb, "and I want so many answering needles." And of both brother and sister it may be said that their likes wore as well as most people's loves.

Mary Anne Lamb was born in Crown Office Row, Inner Temple, on the 3d of December, 1764, — year of Hogarth's death. She was the third, as Charles was the youngest, of seven children, all of whom died in infancy, save these two and an elder brother John, her senior by two years. One little sister, Elizabeth, who came when Mary was four years old, lived long enough to imprint an image on the child's memory which, helped by a few relics, remained for life. "The little cap with white satin ribbon grown yellow with long keeping, and a lock of light hair," wrote Mary when she was near sixty, "always brought her pretty, fair face to my view, so that to this day I seem to have a perfect recollection of her features."

The family of the Lambs came originally from Stamford in Lincolnshire, as Charles himself once told a correspondent. Nothing else is known of Mary's ancestry; nor yet even the birth-place or earliest circumstances of John Lamb, the father. If, however, we may accept on Mr. Cowden-Clarke's authority, corroborated by internal evidence, the little story of *Susan Yates*, contributed by Charles to *Mrs. Leicester's School*, as embodying some of his father's earliest recollections, he was born of parents "in no very affluent circumstances," in a lonely part of the fen country, seven miles from the nearest church, an occasional visit to which, "just to see how *goodness thrived*," was a feat to be remembered, such bad and dangerous walking was it in the fens in those days, "a mile as good as four." What is quite certain is that while John Lamb was still a child his family removed to Lincoln, with means so straitened that he was sent to service in London. Whether his father were dead, or, sadder still, in a lunatic asylum — since we are told with emphasis that the hereditary seeds of madness in the Lamb family came from the father's side,—it is beyond doubt that misfortune of some kind must have been the cause of the child's being sent thus prematurely to earn his bread in service. His subsequently becoming a barrister's clerk seems to indicate that his early nurture and education had been of a gentler kind than this rough thrusting out into the world of a mere child would otherwise imply : in confirmation of which it is to be noted that afterwards, in the dark crisis of family misfortune, "an old gentlewoman of fortune" appears on the scene as a relative.

In spite of early struggles John Lamb grew up

> A merry, cheerful man.   A merrier man,
> A man more apt to frame matter for mirth,
> Mad jokes and antics for a Christmas-eve,
> Making life social and the laggard time
> To move on nimbly, never yet did cheer
> The little circle of domestic friends.

Inflexibly honest and upright, too, with a dash of chivalry in his nature. Who is not familiar with his portrait as "Lovel" in *The Benchers of the Inner Temple?* Elizabeth, his wife, a native of Ware, whose maiden name was Field, was many years younger than himself. She was a handsome, dignified-looking woman; like her husband, fond of pleasure; a good and affectionate mother, also, in the main, yet lacking insight into the characters of her children — into Mary's, at any rate, towards whom she never manifested that maternal tenderness which makes the heart wise whatever the head may be. Mary, a shy, sensitive, nervous, affectionate child, who early showed signs of a liability to brain disorder, above all things needed tender and judicious care. "Her mother loved her," wrote Charles, in after years, "as she loved us all, with a mother's love; but in opinion, in feeling and sentiment and disposition, bore so distant a resemblance to her daughter that she never understood her right — never could believe how much *she* loved her, — but met her caresses, her protestations of filial affection, too frequently with coldness and repulse. Still she was a good mother. God forbid I should think of her but most respectfully, most affectionately. Yet she would always love my brother above Mary, who was not worthy of one-tenth of that affection which Mary had a right to claim."

John, the eldest, a handsome, lively, active boy, was just what his good looks and his being the favorite were likely to make of a not very happily endowed nature. "Dear, little, selfish, craving John" he was in childhood, and dear, big, selfish John he remained in manhood; treated with tender indulgence by his brother and sister, who cheerfully exonerated him from taking up any share of the burthen of sorrow and privation which became the portion of his family by the time he was grown up and prosperously afloat.

A maiden aunt, a worthy but uncanny old soul, whose odd, silent ways and odder witch-like mutterings and mumblings, coupled with a wild look in her eyes as she peered out from under her spectacles, made her an object of dread rather than love to Mary, as afterwards to Charles, in whom she garnered up her heart, completed the family group, but did not add to its harmony, for she and her sister-in-law ill agreed. They were, in "their different ways," wrote Mary, looking back on childhood from middle-life, "the best creatures in the world; but they set out wrong at first. They made each other miserable for full twenty years of their lives. My mother was a perfect gentle-woman; my aunty as unlike a gentlewoman as you can possibly imagine a good old woman to be; so that my dear mother (who, though you do not know it, is always in my poor head and heart) used to distress and weary her with incessant and unceasing attention and polite-ness to gain her affection. The old woman could not return this in kind and did not know what to make of it — thought it all deceit, and used to hate my mother with a bitter hatred, which, of course, was soon returned with inter-est. A little frankness and looking into each other's characters at first would have spared all this, and they would have lived as they died, fond of each other for the last ten years of their lives. When we grew up and harmonized them a little they sincerely loved each other."

In these early days Mary's was a comfortable though a very modest home; a place of "snug fire-sides, the low-built roof, parlors ten feet by ten, frugal boards, and all the homeliness of home;" a wholesome soil to be planted in, which permitted no helplessness in the practical details of domestic life; above poverty in the actual though not in the conventional sense of the word. Such book-learning as fell to her lot was obtained at a day-school in Fetter Lane, Holborn, where, notwithstanding the inscription over the door, "Mr. William Bird, Teacher of Mathematics and Languages," reading in the mother-tongue, writing and "ciphering" were all that was learned. The school-room looked into a dingy, discolored garden, in the passage leading from Fetter Lane into Bartlett's Buildings; and there boys were taught in the morning and their sisters in the afternoon by "a gentle usher" named Starkey, whose subsequent misfortunes have rescued him and Mary's school-days from oblivion. For, having in his old age drifted into an almshouse at Newcastle, the tale of his wanderings and his woes found its way into print and finally into Hone's *Every Day Book*, where, meeting the eyes of Charles and Mary Lamb, it awakened in both old memories which took shape in the sketch called *Captain Starkey*.

"Poor Starkey, when young, had that peculiar stamp of old-fashionedness in his face which makes it impossible for a beholder to predict any particular age in the object : you can scarce make a guess between seventeen and seven-and-thirty. This antique cast always seems to promise ill luck and penury. Yet it seems he was not always the abject thing he came to. My sister, who well remembers him, can hardly forgive Mr. Thomas Ranson for making an etching so unlike her idea of him when he was at Mr. Bird's school. Old age and poverty, a life-long poverty, she thinks, could at no time have effaced the marks of native gentility which were once so visible in a face otherwise strikingly ugly, thin and careworn. From her recollections of him, she thinks he would have wanted bread before he would have begged or borrowed a halfpenny. 'If any of the girls,' she says, 'who were my school-fellows should be reading through their aged spectacles tidings from the dead of their youthful friend Starkey, they will feel a pang as I do at having teased his gentle spirit.'

"They were big girls, it seems, too old to attend his instructions with the silence necessary ; and, however old age and a long state of beggary seems to have reduced his writing faculties to a state of imbecility, in those days his language occasionally rose to the bold and figurative, for, when he was in despair to stop their chattering, his ordinary phrase was, ' Ladies, if you will not hold your peace, not all the powers in heaven can make you.' Once he was missing for a day or two ; he had run away. A little, old, unhappy-looking man brought him back — it was his father, and he did no business in the school that day, but sat moping in a corner with his hands before his face ; the girls, his tormentors, in pity for his case, for the rest of the day forbore to annoy him.

" ' I had been there but a few months,' adds she, ' when Starkey, who was the chief instructor of us girls, communicated to us a profound secret, that the tragedy of Cato was shortly to be acted by the elder boys, and that we were to be invited to the representation.' That Starkey lent a helping hand in fashioning the actors, she remembers ; and, but for his unfortunate person, he might have had some distinguished part in the scene to enact. As it was, he had the arduous task of prompter assigned to him, and his feeble voice was heard clear and distinct repeat-

ing the text during the whole performance.
She describes her recollection of the cast of
characters even now with a relish : Martia, by
the handsome Edgar Hickman, who afterwards
went to Africa, and of whom she never afterwards heard tidings ; Lucia, by Master Walker,
whose sister was her particular friend ; Cato, by
John Hunter, a masterly declaimer, but a plain
boy, and shorter by a head than his two sons in
the scene, etc.   In conclusion, Starkey appears
to have been one of those mild spirits which,
not originally deficient in understanding, are
crushed by penury into dejection and feebleness.
He might have proved a useful adjunct, if not
an ornament to society, if fortune had taken
him into a very little fostering ; but wanting
that, he became a captain — a by-word — and
lived and died a broken bulrush."

But the chief and best part of Mary's education was due to the fact that her father's
employer, Mr. Salt, had a good library, "into
which she was tumbled early" and suffered to
"browse there without much selection or prohi-
bition."   A little selection, however, would have
made the pasturage all the wholsomer to a child
of Mary's sensitive, brooding nature ; for the
witch stories and cruel tales of the sufferings of
the martyrs on which she pored all alone, as her
brother did after her, wrought upon her tender

brain and lent their baleful aid to nourish those seeds of madness which she inherited, as may be inferred from a subsequent adventure.

When tripping to and from school or playing in the Temple Gardens Mary must sometimes, though we have no record of the fact, have set eyes on Oliver Goldsmith: for the first ten years of her life were the last of his, spent, though with frequent sojourns elsewhere, in the Temple. And in the Temple churchyard he was buried, just ten months before the birth of Charles.

The London born and bred child had occasional tastes of joyous, healthful life in the country, for her mother had hospitable relatives in her native county, pleasant Hertfordshire. Specially was there a great-aunt married to a substantial yeoman named Gladman, living at Mackery End within a gentle walk of Wheathampstead, the visits to whom remained in Mary's memory as the most delightful recollections of her childhood. In after-life she embodied them, mingling fiction with fact, in a story called *Louisa Manners, or the Farm-house,* where she tells in sweet and child-like words of the ecstasy of a little four-year-old girl on finding herself for the first time in the midst of fields quite full of bright, shining yellow flowers, with sheep and young lambs feeding; of the inexhaustible interest of the farm-yard, the thresher in the barn with his terrifying flail and black beard, the collection of eggs and searching for scarce violets ("if we could find eggs and violets too, what happy children we were"); of the hay-making and the sheep-shearing, the great wood fires and the farm-house suppers.

This will recall to the reader Elia's *Mackery End;* how, forty years afterwards, brother and sister revisited the old farm-house one day in the midst of June, and how Bridget (so he always called Mary in print) "remembered her old acquaintance again ; some altered features, of course, a little grudged at. At first, indeed, she was ready to disbelieve for joy; but the scene soon reconfirmed itself in her affections, and she traversed every out-post of the old mansion, to the wood-house, the orchard, the place where the pigeon-house had stood (house and birds were alike flown), with a breathless impatience of recognition which was more pardonable, perhaps, than decorous at the age of fifty-odd. But Bridget in some things is behind her years."

" . . . The only thing left was to get into the house, and that was a difficulty which to me singly would have been insurmountable, for I am terribly shy in making myself known to strangers and out-of-date kinsfolk. Love,

stronger than scruple, winged my cousin in
without me; but she soon returned with a
creature that might have sat to a sculptor for
the image of Welcome. . . . To have seen
Bridget and her,—it was like the meeting of
the two scriptural cousins! There was a grace
and dignity, an amplitude of form and stature,
answering to her mind in this farmer's wife,
which would have shined in a palace. . . ."

To return to the days of childhood, Mary also
paid visits to her maternal grandmother Field,
housekeeper to the Plumers at their stately but
forsaken mansion of Blakesware; but here the
pleasure was mingled with a kind of weird
solemnity. Mary has left on record her experiences in a tale which forms a sort of pendant to
Blakesmoor in H——shire, by Elia. Her story
is called *Margaret Green, the Young Mahometan,*
also from *Mrs. Leicester's School*, and, apart
from a slight framework of invention ("Mrs.
Beresford," her grandmother, being represented
as the owner instead of housekeeper of the
mansion), is minutely autobiographical. "Every
morning when she (Mrs. Beresford) saw me, she
used to nod her head very kindly and say, 'How
do you do, little Margaret?' But I do not
recollect that she ever spoke to me during the
remainder of the day, except, indeed, after I
had read the psalms and the chapters which

was my daily task ; then she used constantly to observe that I improved in my reading, and frequently added, 'I never heard a child read so distinctly.' When my daily portion of reading was over I had a taste of needlework, which generally lasted half an hour. I was not allowed to pass more time in reading or work, because my eyes were very weak, for which reason I was always set to read in the large-print family Bible. I was very fond of reading, and when I could, unobserved, steal a few minutes as they were intent on their work, I used to delight to read in the historical part of the Bible ; but this, because of my eyes, was a forbidden pleasure, and the Bible being never removed out of the room, it was only for a short time together that I dared softly to lift up the leaves and peep into it. As I was permitted to walk in the garden or wander about the house whenever I pleased, I used to leave the parlor for hours together, and make out my own solitary amusement as well as I could. My first visit was always to a very large hall, which, from being paved with marble, was called the Marble Hall. The heads of the twelve Cæsars were hung round the hall. Every day I mounted on the chairs to look at them and to read the inscriptions underneath, till I became perfectly familiar with their names and features.

Hogarth's prints were below the Cæsars. I
was very fond of looking at them and endeavoring to make out their meaning. An old broken
battledore and some shuttlecocks with most of
the feathers missing were on a marble slab
in one corner of the hall, which constantly
reminded me that there had once been younger
inhabitants here than the old lady and her
gray-headed servants. In another corner stood
a marble figure of a satyr; every day I laid my
hand on his shoulder to feel how cold he was.
This hall opened into a room full of family portraits. They were all in dresses of former
times; some were old men and women, and
some were children. I used to long to have a
fairy's power to call the children down from
their frames to play with me. One little girl
in particular, who hung by the side of the glass
door which opened into the garden, I often
invited to walk there with me; but she still
kept her station, one arm round a little lamb's
neck and in her hand a large bunch of roses.
From this room I usually proceeded to the
garden. When I was weary of the garden I
wandered over the rest of the house. The best
suite of rooms I never saw by any other light
than what glimmered through the tops of the
window-shutters, which, however, served to
show the carved chimney-pieces and the curi-

ous old ornaments about the rooms ; but the worked furniture and carpets of which I had heard such constant praises I could have but an imperfect sight of, peeping under the covers which were kept over them by the dim light ; for I constantly lifted up a corner of the envious cloth that hid these highly-praised rareties from my view.

" The bed-rooms were also regularly explored by me, as well to admire the antique furniture as for the sake of contemplating the tapestry hangings, which were full of Bible history. The subject of the one which chiefly attracted my attention was Hagar and her son Ishmael. Every day I admired the beauty of the youth, and pitied the forlorn state of him and his mother in the wilderness. At the end of the gallery into which these tapestry rooms opened was one door which, having often in vain attempted to open, I concluded to be locked ; and finding myself shut out, I was very desirous of seeing what it contained, and though still foiled in the attempt, I every day endeavored to turn the lock, which, whether by constantly trying I loosened, being probably a very old one, or that the door was not locked, but fastened tight by time, I know not. To my great joy, as I was one day trying the lock as usual, it gave way, and I found myself in this so long-desired room.

"It proved to be a very large library. This was indeed a precious discovery. I looked round on the books with the greatest delight: I thought I would read them every one. I now forsook all my favorite haunts and passed all my time here. I took down first one book, then another. If you never spent whole mornings alone in a large library, you cannot conceive the pleasure of taking down books in the constant hope of finding an entertaining book among them; yet after many days, meeting with nothing but disappointment, it became less pleasant. All the books within my reach were folios of the gravest cast. I could understand very little that I read in them, and the old dark print and the length of the lines made my eyes ache.

"When I had almost resolved to give up the search as fruitless, I perceived a volume lying in an obscure corner of the room. I opened it; it was a charming print; the letters were almost as large as the type of the family Bible. In the first page I looked into I saw the name of my favorite Ishmael, whose face I knew so well from the tapestry and whose history I had often read in the Bible. I sat myself down to read this book with the greatest eagerness. The title of it was *Mahometanism Explained.* . . . A great many of the leaves were torn out, but enough remained to make me imagine that Ish-

mael was the true son of Abraham. I read here
that the true descendants of Abraham were
known by a light which streamed from the middle of their foreheads. It said that Ishmael's
father and mother first saw this light streaming
from his forehead as he was lying asleep in the
cradle. I was very sorry so many of the leaves
were torn out, for it was as entertaining as a
fairy tale. I used to read the history of Ishmael
and then go and look at him in the tapestry, and
then read his history again. When I had
almost learned the history of Ishmael by heart
I read the rest of the book, and then I came to
the history of Mahomet, who was there said to
be the last descendant of Abraham.

"If Ishmael had engaged so much of my
thoughts, how much more so must Mahomet?
His history was full of nothing but wonders
from beginning to end. The book said that
those who believed all the wonderful stories
which were related of Mahomet were called
Mahometans and True Believers; I concluded
that I must be a Mahometan, for I believed
every word I read.

"At length I met with something which I
also believed, though I trembled as I read it.
This was, that after we are dead we are to pass
over a narrow bridge which crosses a bottomless
gulf. The bridge was described to be no wider

than a silken thread, and it is said that all who were not Mahometans would slip on one side of this bridge and drop into the tremendous gulf that had no bottom. I considered myself as a Mahometan, yet I was perfectly giddy whenever I thought of passing over this bridge. One day, seeing the old lady totter across the room, a sudden terror seized me, for I thought how would she ever be able to get over the bridge? Then, too, it was that I first recollected that my mother would also be in imminent danger; for I imagined she had never heard the name of Mahomet, because I foolishly conjectured this book had been locked up for ages in the library and was utterly unknown to the rest of the world.

"All my desire was now to tell them the discovery I had made; for, I thought, when they knew of the existence of *Mahometanism Explained* they would read it and become Mahometans to insure themselves a safe passage over the silken bridge. But it wanted more courage than I possessed to break the matter to my intended converts; I must acknowledge that I had been reading without leave; and the habit of never speaking or being spoken to considerably increased the difficulty.

"My anxiety on this subject threw me into a fever. I was so ill that my mother thought it

necessary to sleep in the same room with me.
In the middle of the night I could not resist the
strong desire I felt to tell her what preyed so
much on my mind.

"I awoke her out of a sound sleep and begged
she would be so kind as to be a Mahometan. She
was very much alarmed, for she thought I was
delirious, which I believe I was : for I tried to
explain the reason of my request, but it was in
such an incoherent manner that she could not
at all comprehend what I was talking about.
The next day a physician was sent for, and he
discovered, by several questions that he put to
me, that I had read myself into a fever. He
gave me medicines and ordered me to be kept
very quiet, and said he hoped in a few days I
should be very well ; but as it was a new case
to him, he never having attended a little Mahometan before, if any lowness continued after
he had removed the fever he would, with my
mother's permission, take me home with him to
study this extraordinary case at his leisure ; and
added that he could then hold a consultation with
his wife, who was often very useful to him in pre-
scribing remedies for the maladies of his younger
patients."

In the sequel, this sensible and kindly doctor
takes his little patient home, and restores her
by giving her child-like, wholesome pleasures

and rational sympathy. I fear that this only shadowed forth the wise tenderness with which Mary Lamb would have treated such a child rather than what befell herself; and that with the cruelty of ignorance Mary's mother and grandmother suffered her young spirit to do battle still, in silence and inward solitariness, with the phantoms imagination conjured up in her too-sensitive brain. "Polly, what are those poor, crazy, moythered brains of yours thinking always?" was worthy Mrs. Field's way of endeavoring to win the confidence of the thoughtful, suffering child. The words in the story "my mother almost wholly discontinued talking to me," "I scarcely ever heard a word addressed to me from morning to night," have a ring of truth, of bitter experience in them, which makes the heart ache. Yet it was no result of sullenness on either side; least of all did it breed any ill feeling on Mary's. It was simple stupidity, lack of insight or sympathy in the elders; and on hers was repaid by the sweetest affection, and, in after years, by a self-sacrificing devotion which, carried at last far beyond her strength, led to the great calamity of her life. Grandmother Field was a fine old character, however, as the reader of *Elia* well knows. She had

> A mounting spirit, one that entertained
> Scorn of base action, deed dishonorable
> Or aught unseemly.

Like her daughter, Mrs. Lamb, she had been a handsome, stately woman in her prime, and when bent with age and pain (for she suffered with a cruel malady), cheerful patience and fortitude gave her dignity of another and higher kind. But, like her daughter, she seems to have been wanting in those finer elements of tenderness and sympathy which were of vital consequence in the rearing up of a child smitten like Mary with a hereditary tendency to madness.

CHAPTER II.

1775 – 1796. — Æt. 11 – 32.

On the 10th of February, 1775, arrived a new member into the household group in Crown Office Row — Charles, the child of his father's old age, the "weakly but very pretty babe" who was to prove their strong support. And now Mary was no longer a lonely girl. She was just old enough to be trusted to nurse and tend the baby, and she became a mother to it. In after-life she spoke of the comfort, the wholesome, curative influence upon her young troubled mind, which this devotion to Charles in his infancy brought with it. And as he grew older rich was her reward ; for he repaid the debt with a love half filial, half fraternal, than which no human tie was ever stronger or more sublimely adequate to the strain of a terrible emergency. As his young mind unfolded he found in her intelligence and love the same genial, fostering influences that had cherished his feeble frame into health and strength. It was with his little hand in hers that he first trod the Temple gardens, and spelled out the inscriptions on the sun-dials and on the tomb-stones in the old burying-ground, and wondered, finding only lists of the virtues, "where all the naughty people were buried?" Like Mary, his disposition was so different from that of his gay, pleasure-loving parents that they but ill understood "and gave themselves little trouble about him," which also tended to draw brother and sister closer together. There are no other records of Mary's girlhood than such as may be gathered from the story of her brother's early life ; of how, when he was five and she was fifteen, she came near to losing him from small-pox, Aunt Hetty grieving over him, "the only thing in the world she loved," as she was wont to say, with a mother's tears. And how, three years later (in 1782), she had to give up his daily companionship and see him, now grown a handsome boy with "crisply curling black hair, clear brown complexion, aquiline, slightly Jewish cast of features, winning smile, and glittering, restless eyes," equipped as a Christ's Hospital boy, and, with Aunt Hetty, to

> . . . peruse him round and round,
> And hardly know him in his yellow coats,
> Red leathern belt and gown of russet blue.

Coleridge was already a Blue Coat boy, but older and too high above Charles in the school for comradeship then. To Lamb, with home close at hand, it was a happy time ; but Coleridge, homeless and friendless in the great city, had no mitigations of the rough Spartan discipline which prevailed ; and the weekly whole holidays when, turned adrift in the streets from morn till night, he had nothing but a crust of bread in his pockets, and no resource but to beguile the pangs of hunger in summer with hours of bathing in the New River, and in winter with furtive hanging round book-stalls, wrought permanent harm to his fine-strung organization. Nor did the gentleness of his disposition or the brilliancy of his powers save him from the birch-loving brutalities of old Boyer, who was wont to add an extra stripe "because he was so ugly."

In the Lamb household the domestic outlook grew dark as soon as Mary was grown up, for her father's faculties and her mother's health failed early ; and when, in his fifteenth year, Charles left Christ's Hospital, it was already needful for him to take up the burthens of a man on his young shoulders ; and for Mary not only to make head against sickness, helplessness, old age, with its attendant exigencies, but to add to the now straitened means by taking in millinery work.

For eleven years, as she has told us, she maintained herself by the needle ; from the age of twenty-one to thirty-two, that is. It was not in poor old Aunt Hetty's nature to be helpful either. "She was from morning till night poring over good books and devotional exercises. . . . The only secular employment I remember to have seen her engaged in was the splitting of French beans and dropping them into a basin of fair water," says Elia. Happily a clerkship in the South Sea House, where his brother already was, enabled Charles to maintain his parents, and a better post in the India House was obtained two years afterwards. Nor were there wanting snatches of pleasant holiday, sometimes shared by Mary. Of one, a visit to the sea, there is a beautiful reminiscence in *The Old Margate Hoy*, written more than thirty years afterwards. "It was our first sea-side experiment," he says, "and many circumstances combined to make it the most agreeable holiday of my life. We had neither of us seen the sea" (he was fifteen and Mary twenty-six), "and we had never been from home so long together in company." The disappointment they both felt at the first sight of the sea he explains with one of his subtle and profound suggestions. "Is it not," . . . says he, "that we had expected to behold (absurdly I grant, but by the law of imagination inevitably) not a definite object compassable by the eye, but *all the sea at once, the commensurate antagonist of the earth?* Whereas the eye can take in a 'slip of salt water.'" The whole passage is one of Elia's finest.

Then Coleridge, too, who had remained two years longer at Christ's Hospital than Lamb, and after he went up to Cambridge in 1791, continued to pay frequent visits to London, spent many a glorious evening, not only those memorable ones with Charles in the parlor of the "Salutation and Cat," but in his home; and was not slow to discover Mary's fine qualities and to take her into his brotherly heart, as a little poem, written so early as 1794, to cheer his friend during a serious illness of hers, testifies: —

> Cheerily, dear Charles!
> Thou thy best friend shalt cherish many a year,
> Such warm presages feel I of high hope.
> For not uninterested the dear maid
> I've viewed — her soul affectionate yet wise,
> Her polished wit as mild as lambent glories
> That play around a sainted infant's head.

The year 1795 witnessed changes for all. The father, now wholly in his dotage, was pensioned off by Mr. Salt, and the family had to exchange their old home in the Temple for straitened

lodgings in Little Queen street, Holborn (the
site of which and of the adjoining houses is now
occupied by Trinity Church). Coleridge, too,
had left Cambridge and was at Bristol, drawn
thither by his newly-formed friendship with
Southey, lecturing, writing, dreaming of his
ideal Pantisocracy on the banks of the Susque-
hannah, and love-making. The love-making
ended in marriage the autumn of that same
year. Meanwhile Lamb, too, was first tasting
the joys and sorrows of love. Alice W——
lingers but as a shadow in the records of his
life : the passion, however, was real enough and
took deep hold of him, conspiring with the cares
and trials of home-life, unrelieved now by the
solace of Coleridge's society, to give a fatal stimulus to the germs of brain-disease, which were
part of the family heritage, and for six weeks he
was in a mad-house. "In your absence," he
tells his friend afterwards, "the tide of melancholy rushed in and did its worst mischief by
overwhelming my reason." Who can doubt the
memory of this attack strengthened the bond of
sympathy between Mary and himself, and gave
him a fellow-feeling for her no amount of affection alone could have realized? As in her case,
too, the disordered took the form of a great
heightening and intensifying of the imaginative
faculty. "I look back on it at times," wrote he

after his recovery, "with a gloomy kind of envy; for while it lasted I had many, many hours of pure happiness. Dream not, Coleridge, of having tasted all the grandeur and wildness of fancy till you have gone mad. . . The sonnet I send you has small merit as poetry, but you will be curious to read it when I tell you it was written in my prison-house in one of my lucid intervals : —

TO MY SISTER.

If from my lips some angry accents fell,
Peevish complaint, or harsh reproof unkind,
'Twas but the error of a sickly mind
And troubled thoughts, clouding the purer well
And waters clear of Reason; and for me
Let this my verse the poor atonement be —
My verse, which thou to praise wert e'er inclined
Too highly, and with a partial eye to see
No blemish. Thou to me didst ever show
Kindest affection; and would oft-times lend
An ear to the desponding love-sick lay,
Weeping my sorrows with me, who repay
But ill the mighty debt of love I owe,
Mary, to thee, my sister and my friend.

No sooner was Charles restored to himself than the elder brother, John, met with a serious accident; and though whilst in health he had carried himself and his earnings to more comfortable quarters, he did not now fail to return and be nursed with anxious solicitude by his brother and sister. This was the last ounce. Mary, worn out with years of nightly as well as daily attendance upon her mother, who was now wholly deprived of the use of her limbs, and harassed by a close application to needlework to help her, in which she had been obliged to take a young apprentice, was at last strained beyond the utmost pitch of physical endurance, "worn down to a state of extreme nervous misery." About the middle of September, she being then thirty-two years old, her family observed some symptoms of insanity in her, which had so much increased by the 21st that her brother early in the morning went to Dr. Pitcairn, who, unhappily, was out. On the afternoon of that day, seized with a sudden attack of frenzy, she snatched a knife from the table and pursued the young apprentice round the room, when her mother, interposing, received a fatal stab and died instantly. Mary was totally unconscious of what she had done ; Aunt Hetty fainted with terror ; the father was too feeble in mind for any but a confused and transient impression. It was Charles alone who confronted all the anguish and horror of the scene. With the stern brevity of deep emotion he wrote to Coleridge five days afterwards : —

"My poor, dear, dearest sister, in a fit of insanity, has been the death of her own mother.

I was at hand only time enough to snatch the knife out of her grasp. She is at present in a mad-house, from whence I fear she must be moved to a hospital. God has preserved to me my senses; I eat, and drink, and sleep, and have my judgment, I believe, very sound. My poor father was slightly wounded, and I am left to take care of him and my aunt. Mr. Norris of the Blue Coat School has been very kind to us, and we have no other friend; but, thank God, I am very calm and composed, and able to do the best that remains to do. Write as religious a letter as possible, but no mention of what is gone and done with. With me 'the former things are passed away,' and I have something more to do than to feel. God Almighty have us all in His keeping! Mention nothing of poetry. I have destroyed every vestige of past vanities of that kind. . . Your own judgment will convince you not to take any notice of this yet to your dear wife. You look after your family; I have my reason and strength left to take care of mine. I charge you, don't think of coming to see me. Write. I will not see you if you come. God Almighty love you and all of us!"

Coleridge responded to this appeal for sympathy and comfort by the following — the only letter of his to Lamb which has been preserved: —

"Your letter, my friend, struck me with a mighty horror. It rushed upon me and stupefied my feelings. You bid me write you a religious letter; I am not a man who would attempt to insult the greatness of your anguish by any other consolation. Heaven knows that in the easiest fortunes there is much dissatisfaction and weariness of spirit; much that calls for the exercise of patience and resignation; but in storms like these, that shake the dwelling and make the heart tremble, there is no middle way between despair and the yielding up of the whole spirit to the guidance of faith. And surely it is a matter of joy that your faith in Jesus has been preserved; the Comforter that should relieve you is not far from you. But as you are a Christian, in the name of that Saviour who was filled with bitterness and made drunken with wormwood, I conjure you to have recourse in frequent prayer to 'his God and your God,' the God of mercies and Father of all comfort. Your poor father is, I hope, almost senseless of the calamity; the unconscious instrument of Divine Providence knows it not, and your mother is in Heaven. It is sweet to be roused from a frightful dream by the song of birds and the gladsome rays of the morning. Ah, how infinitely more sweet to be awakened from the blackness and amazement of a sudden horror by

the glories of God manifest, and the hallelujahs
of angels !

"As to what regards yourself, I approve altogether of your abandoning what you justly call
vanities. I look upon you as a man called by
sorrow and anguish and a strange desolation of
hopes into quietness, and a soul set apart and
made peculiar to God ; we cannot arrive at any
portion of heavenly bliss without, in some
measure, imitating Christ. And they arrive at
the largest inheritance who imitate the most
difficult parts of his character, and, bowed down
and crushed under foot, cry, in fullness of faith,
'Father, Thy will be done.'

"I wish above measure to have you for a
little while here ; no visitants shall blow on the
nakedness of your feelings ; you shall be quiet,
that your spirit may be healed. I see no possible objection, unless your father's helplessness
prevent you and unless you are necessary to
him. If this be not the case, I charge you
write me that you will come.

"I charge you, my dearest friend, not to dare
to encourage gloom or despair ; you are a temporary sharer in human miseries, that you may
be an eternal partaker of the divine nature. I
charge you, if by any means it be possible,
come to me."

How the storm was weathered, with what

2

mingled fortitude and sweetness Lamb sustained
the wrecked household and rescued his sister,
when reason returned, from the living death of
perpetual confinement in a mad-house, must be
read in the answer to Coleridge : —

"Your letter was an inestimable treasure to
me. It will be a comfort to you, I know, to
know that our prospects are somewhat brighter.
My poor, dear, dearest sister, the unhappy and
unconscious instrument of the Almighty's
judgment on our house, is restored to her
senses ; to a dreadful sense and recollection of
what has passed, awful to her mind, and impressive (as it must be to the end of life), but
tempered with religious resignation and the
reasonings of a sound judgment, which in this
early stage knows how to distinguish between
a deed committed in a transient fit of frenzy
and the terrible guilt of a mother's murder. I
have seen her. I found her this morning, calm
and serene ; far, very far from an indecent, for-
getful serenity. She has a most affectionate
and tender concern for what has happened. Indeed, from the beginning — frightful and hopeless as her disorder seemed — I had confidence
enough in her strength of mind and religious
principle to look forward to a time when even
she might recover tranquillity. God be praised,
Coleridge! wonderful as it is to tell, I have

never once been otherwise than collected and calm; even on the dreadful day, and in the midst of the terrible scene, I preserved a tranquillity which bystanders may have construed into indifference; a tranquillity not of despair. Is it folly or sin in me to say that it was a religious principle that most supported me? I allow much to other favorable circumstances. I felt that I had something else to do than to regret. On that first evening my aunt was lying insensible — to all appearance like one dying; my father, with his poor forehead plastered over from a wound he had received from a daughter dearly loved by him and who loved him no less dearly; my mother a dead and murdered corpse in the next room; yet I was wonderfully supported. I closed not my eyes in sleep that night, but lay without terrors and without despair. I have lost no sleep since. I had been long used not to rest in things of sense; had endeavored after a comprehension of mind unsatisfied with the 'ignorant present time,' and this kept me up. I had the whole weight of the family thrown on me; for my brother, little disposed (I speak not without tenderness for him) at any time to take care of old age and infirmities, had now, with his bad leg, an exemption from such duties, and I was left alone.

"One little incident may serve to make you understand my way of managing my mind. Within a day or two after the fatal one we dressed for dinner a tongue, which we had had salted for some weeks in the house. As I sat down a feeling like remorse struck me; this tongue poor Mary got for me, and can I partake of it now when she is far away? A thought occurred and relieved me; if I give in to this way of feeling, there is not a chair, a room, an object in our rooms, that will not awaken the keenest griefs. I must rise above such weaknesses. I hope this was not want of true feeling. I did not let this carry me, though, too far. On the very second day (I date from the day of horrors), as is usual in such cases, there were a matter of twenty people, I do think, supping in our room; they prevailed on me to eat *with them* (for to eat I never refused). They were all making merry in the room! Some had come from friendship, some from busy curiosity and some from interest. I was going to partake with them, when my recollection came that my poor dead mother was lying in the next room — the very next room; a mother who, through life, wished nothing but her children's welfare. Indignation, the rage of grief, something like remorse, rushed upon my mind. In an agony of emotion I found my way mechanically to the adjoining room and fell on my knees by the side of her coffin, asking forgiveness of Heaven and sometimes of her for forgetting her so soon. Tranquillity returned and it was the only violent emotion that mastered me. I think it did me good.

"I mention these things because I hate concealment and love to give a faithful journal of what passes within me. Our friends have been very good. Sam Le Grice [an old schoolfellow well known to the readers of Lamb], who was then in town, was with me the first three or four days and was as a brother to me ; gave up every hour of his time, to the very hurting of his health and spirits, in constant attendance and humoring my poor father ; talked with him, read to him, played at cribbage with him, (for so short is the old man's recollection that he was playing at cards as though nothing had happened while the coroner's inquest was sitting over the way !) Samuel wept tenderly when he went away, for his mother wrote him a very severe letter on his loitering so long in town, and he was forced to go. Mr. Norris, of Christ's Hospital, has been as a father to me ; Mrs. Norris as a mother ; though we had few claims on them. A gentleman, brother to my godmother, from whom we never had right or reason to expect any such assistance, sent my father twenty

pounds ; and to crown all these God's blessings
to our family at such a time, an old lady, a
cousin of my father and aunt, a gentlewoman of
fortune, is to take my aunt and make her comfortable for the short remainder of her days.
My aunt is recovered and as well as ever, and
highly pleased at the thought of going, and has
generously given up the interest of her little
money (which was formerly paid my father for
her board) wholly and solely to my sister's use.
Reckoning this we have, Daddy and I, for our
two selves and an old maid-servant to look after
him when I am out, which will be necessary,
£170 (or £180 rather) a year, out of which we
can spare £50 or £60 at least, for Mary while
she stays at Islington, where she must and
shall stay during her father's life, for his and
her comfort. I know John will make speeches
about it, but she shall not go into a hospital.
The good lady of the mad-house, and her
daughter, an elegant, sweet-behaved young
lady, love her and are taken with her amazingly ; and I know from her own mouth she loves
them and longs to be with them as much. Poor
thing, they say she was but the other morning
saying she knew she must go to Bethlem for
life ; that one of her brothers would have it so,
but the other would wish it not, but be obliged
to go with the stream ; that she had often, as

she passed Bethlem, thought it likely, 'Here it may be my fate to end my days,' conscious of a certain flightiness in her poor head oftentimes, and mindful of more than one severe illness of that nature before. A legacy of £100 which my father will have at Christmas, and this £20 I mentioned before, with what is in the house, will much more than set us clear. If my father, an old servant-maid and I can't live and live comfortably on £130 or £120 a year, we ought to burn by slow fires, and I almost would that Mary might not go into a hospital. Let me not leave one unfavorable impression on your mind respecting my brother. Since this has happened he has been very kind and brotherly ; but I fear for his mind : he has taken his ease in the world and is not fit to struggle with difficulties, nor has he much accustomed himself to throw himself into their way, and I know his language is already, ' Charles, you must take care of yourself ; you must not abridge yourself of a single pleasure you have been used to,' etc., etc., and in that style of talking. But you, a necessarian, can respect a difference of mind and love what is amiable in a character not perfect. He has been very good, but I fear for his mind. Thank God, I can unconnect myself with him, and shall manage all my father's moneys in future myself if I take charge of Daddy, which poor John has not even hinted a wish at any future time even to share with me. The lady at this mad-house assures me that I may dismiss immediately both doctor and apothecary, retaining occasionally a composing draught or so for a while; and there is a less expensive establishment in her house, where she will not only have a room but a nurse to herself for £50 or guineas a year — the outside would be £60. You know by economy how much more even I shall be able to spare for her comforts. She will, I fancy, if she stays, make one of the family rather than one of the patients; and the old and young ladies I like exceedingly and she loves them dearly; and they, as the saying is, take to her very extraordinarily, if it is extraordinary that people who see my sister should love her. Of all the people I ever saw in the world, my poor sister was most and thoroughly devoid of the least tincture of selfishness. I will enlarge upon her qualities, poor, dear, dearest soul, in a future letter for my own comfort, for I understand her thoroughly; and, if I mistake not, in the most trying situation that a human being can be found in, she will be found (I speak not with sufficient humility, I fear); but humanly and foolishly speaking, she will be found, I trust, uniformly great and amiable."

The depth and tenderness of Mary's but half-requited love for her mother, and the long years of daily and nightly devotion to her which had borne witness to it and been the immediate cause of the catastrophe, took the sting out of her grief and gave her an unfaltering sense of innocence. They even shed round her a peaceful atmosphere which veiled from her mind's eye the dread scene in all its naked horror, as it would seem from Lamb's next letter : —

"Mary continues serene and cheerful. I have not by me a little letter she wrote to me; for though I see her almost every day, yet we delight to write to one another, for we can see each other but in company with some of the people of the house. I have not the letter by me, but will quote from memory what she wrote in it : 'I have no bad, terrifying dreams. At midnight, when I happen to awake, the nurse sleeping by the side of me, with the noise of the poor mad people around me, I have no fear. The spirit of my mother seems to descend and smile upon me and bid me live to enjoy the life and reason which the Almighty has given me. I shall see her again in Heaven; she will then understand me better. My grandmother, too, will understand me better, and will then say no more, as she used to do, 'Polly, what are

those poor, crazy, moythered brains of yours
thinking of always?' "

And again, in another of her little letters,
not itself preserved, but which Charles trans-
lated "almost literally," he tells us, into verse,
she said : —

> Thou and I, dear friend,
> With filial recognition sweet, shall know
> One day the face of our dear mother in Heaven ;
> And her remembered looks of love shall greet
> With answering looks of love, her placid smiles
> Meet with a smile as placid, and her hand
> With drops of fondness wet, nor fear repulse.

And after speaking, in words already quoted, of
how his mother "had never understood Mary
right," Lamb continues : —

"Every act of duty and of love she could pay,
every kindness (and I speak true when I say to
the hurting of her health, and most probably in
a great part to the derangement of her senses),
through a long course of infirmities and sickness, she could show her, she ever did." "I
will some day, as I promised, enlarge to you
upon my sister's excellences ; 'twill seem like
exaggeration, but I will do it."

Although Mary's recovery had been rapid, to
be permitted to return home was, for the present,
out of the question ; so, cheered by constant

intercourse with Charles, she set herself, with characteristic sweetness, to make the best of life in a private lunatic asylum. "I have satisfaction," Charles tells his unfailing sympathizer, Coleridge, "in being able to bid you rejoice with me in my sister's continued reason and composedness of mind. Let us both be thankful for it. I continue to visit her very frequently, and the people of the house are vastly indulgent to her. She is likely to be as comfortably situated in all respects as those who pay twice or thrice the sum. They love her, and she loves them and makes herself very useful to them. Benevolence sets out on her journey with a good heart and puts a good face on it, but is apt to limp and grow feeble unless she calls in the aid of self-interest by way of crutch. In Mary's case, as far as respects those she is with, 'tis well that these principles are so likely to coöperate. I am rather at a loss sometimes for books for her ; our reading is somewhat confined and we have nearly exhausted our London library. She has her hands too full of work to read much, but a little she must read, for reading was her daily bread."

So wore away the remaining months of this dark year. Perhaps they were loneliest and saddest for Charles. There was no one now to share with him the care of his old father; and second childhood draws unsparingly on the debt of filial affection and gratitude. Cheeringly and ungrudgingly did he pay it. His chief solace was the correspondence with Coleridge; and as his spirits recovered their tone, the mutual discussion of the poems which the two friends were about to publish, conjointly with some of Charles Lloyd's, was resumed. The little volume was to be issued by Cottle, of Bristol, early in the coming year, 1797; and Lamb was desirous to seize the occasion of giving his sister an unlooked-for pleasure and of consecrating his verses by a renouncement and a dedication.

"I have a dedication in my head," he writes, "for my few things, which I want to know if you approve of and can insert. I mean to inscribe them to my sister. It will be unexpected and it will give her pleasure; or do you think it will look whimsical at all? As I have not spoken to her about it I can easily reject the idea. But there is a monotony in the affections which people living together, or, as we do now, very frequently seeing each other, are apt to get into; a sort of indifference in the expression of kindness for each other, which demands that we should sometimes call to our aid the trickery of surprise. The title-page to stand thus:—

POEMS
BY
CHARLES LAMB, OF THE INDIA HOUSE.

Motto:—

> This beauty, in the blossom of my youth,
> When my first fire knew no adulterate incense,
> Nor I no way to flatter but my fondness,
> In the best language my true tongue could tell me,
> And all the broken sighs my sick heart lend me,
> I sued and served.   Long did I love this lady.
>
> *—Massinger.*

The Dedication:—

THE FEW FOLLOWING POEMS,
CREATURES OF THE FANCY AND THE FEELING,
IN LIFE'S MORE VACANT HOURS,
PRODUCED, FOR THE MOST PART, BY
LOVE IN IDLENESS,
ARE,
WITH ALL A BROTHER'S FONDNESS,
INSCRIBED TO
MARY ANNE LAMB,
THE AUTHOR'S BEST FRIEND AND SISTER.

"This is the pomp and paraphernalia of parting, with which I take my leave of a passion which has reigned so royally, so long, within me.   Thus, with its trappings of laureateship, I fling it off, pleased and satisfied with myself that the weakness troubles me no longer.   I am wedded, Coleridge, to the fortunes of my sister and my poor old father. Oh, my friend! I think sometimes, could I recall the days that are past, which among them should I choose? Not those merrier days, not the pleasant days of hope, not those wanderings with a fair-haired maid which I have so often and so feelingly regretted, but the days, Coleridge, of a *mother's* fondness for her *school-boy.* What would I give to call her back to earth for *one* day! — on my knees to ask her pardon for all those little asperities of temper which, from time to time, have given her gentle spirit pain! and the day, my friend, I trust will come. There will be 'time enough' for kind offices of love, if Heaven's 'eternal year' be ours. Hereafter her meek spirit shall not reproach me. Oh! my friend, cultivate the filial feelings! and let no man think himself released from the kind 'charities' of relationship: these shall give him peace at last; these are the best foundation for every species of benevolence. I rejoice to hear by certain channels that you, my friend, are reconciled with all your relations. 'Tis the most kindly and natural species of love, and we have all the associated train of early feelings to secure its strength and perpetuity."

CHAPTER III.

1797–1801. — Æt. 33–37.

AUNT HETTY did not find her expectations of
a comfortable home realized under the roof of
the gentlewoman, who proved herself a typical
rich relation, and wrote to Charles at the beginning of the new year that she found her aged
cousin indolent and mulish, "and that her at-
tachment to us" (he is telling Coleridge the
tale, to whom he could unburthen his heart on
all subjects, sure of sympathy) "is so strong
that she can never be happy apart. The lady
with delicate irony remarks that if I am not a
hypocrite I shall rejoice to receive her again;
and that it will be a means of making me more
fond of home to have so dear a friend to come
home to! The fact is, she is jealous of my
aunt's bestowing any kind recollections on us

while she enjoys the patronage of her roof. She says she finds it inconsistent with her own 'ease and tranquillity' to keep her any longer; and, in fine, summons me to fetch her home. Now, much as I should rejoice to transplant the poor old creature from the chilling air of such patronage, yet I know how straitened we are already, how unable already to answer any demand which sickness or any extraordinary expense may make. I know this; and all unused as I am to struggle with perplexities, I am somewhat nonplussed, to say no worse."

Hetty Lamb found a refuge and a welcome in the old humble home again. But she returned only to die; and Mary was not there to nurse her. She was still in the asylum at Islington, and was indeed herself at this time recovering from an attack of scarlet fever, or something akin to it.

Early in January, 1797, Lamb wrote to Coleridge:— "You and Sara are very good to think so kindly and favorably of poor Mary. I would to God all did so too. But I very much fear she must not think of coming home in my father's lifetime. It is very hard upon her, but our circumstances are peculiar, and we must submit to them. God be praised she is so well as she is. She bears her situation as one who has no right to complain. My poor old aunt,

whom you have seen, the kindest, goodest creature to me when I was at school, who used to
toddle there to bring me good things, when I,
school-boy like, only despised her for it, and
used to be ashamed to see her come and sit herself down on the old coal-hole steps as you went
into the old Grammar School, and open her
apron and bring out her basin with some nice
thing she had caused to be saved for me, — the
good old creature is now lying on her death-
bed. I cannot bear to think on her deplorable
state. To the shock she received on that our
evil day, from which she never completely
recovered, I impute her illness. She says, poor
thing, she is glad she is come home to die with
me ; I was always her favorite."

She lingered a month, and then went to
occupy

> " . . . the same grave-bed
> Where the dead mother lies.
> Oh, my dear mother ! oh, thou dear dead saint !
> Where's now that placid face, where oft hath sat
> A mother's smile to think her son should thrive
> In this bad world when she was dead and gone ?
> And where a tear hath sat (take shame, O son !)
> When that same child hath proved himself unkind.
> One parent yet is left — a wretched thing,
> A sad survivor of his buried wife,
> A palsy-smitten, childish, old, old man,
> A semblance most forlorn of what he was."

"I own I am thankful that the good creature has ended her days of suffering and infirmity," says Lamb to Coleridge. "Good God! who could have foreseen all this but four months back! I had reckoned, in particular, on my aunt's living many years; she was a very hearty old woman. . . . But she was a mere skeleton before she died; looked more like a corpse that had lain weeks in the grave than one fresh dead."

"I thank you, from my heart I thank you," Charles again wrote to Coleridge, "for your solicitude about my sister. She is quite well, but must not, I fear, come to live with us yet a good while. In the first place, because it would hurt her and hurt my father for them to be together; secondly, from a regard to the world's good report, for I fear tongues will be busy whenever that event takes place. Some have hinted, one man has pressed it on me, that she should be in perpetual confinement. What she hath done to deserve, or the necessity of such a hardship, I see not; do you?"

At length Lamb determined to grapple, on Mary's behalf, with the difficulties and embarrassments of the situation. "Painful doubts were suggested," says Talfourd, "by the authorities of the parish where the terrible occurrence happened, whether they were not bound to

institute proceedings which must have placed
her for life at the disposition of the Crown,
especially as no medical assurance could be
given against the probable recurrence of dangerous frenzy. But Charles came to her deliv-
erance ; he satisfied all the parties who had
power to oppose her release, by his solemn
engagement that he would take her under his
care for life ; and he kept his word. Whether
any communication with the Home Secretary
occurred before her release, I have been unable
to ascertain. It was the impression of Mr.
Lloyd, from whom my own knowledge of the
circumstances, which the letters did not con-
tain, was derived, that a communication took
place, on which a similar pledge was given. At
all events the result was that she left the asylum and took up her abode," not with her
brother yet, but in lodgings near him and her
father.

He writes to Coleridge, April 7, 1797 : " Lloyd
may have told you about my sister. . . . If not,
I have taken her out of her confinement, and
taken a room for her at Hackney, and spend my
Sundays, holidays, etc., with her. She boards
herself. In a little half-year's illness and in such
an illness, of such a nature and of such consequences, to get her out into the world again,
with a prospect of her never being so ill again

—this is to be ranked not among the common
blessings of Providence. May that merciful
God make tender my heart and make me as
thankful as, in my distress, I was earnest in my
prayers. Congratulate me on an ever-present
and never-alienable friend like her, and do, do
insert, if you have not *lost*, my dedication [to
Mary]. It will have lost half its value by coming so late." And of another sonnet to her,
which he desires to have inserted, he says : "I
wish to accumulate perpetuating tokens of my
affection to poor Mary."

Two events which brightened this sad year
must not be passed over, though Mary, the
sharer of all her brother's joys and sorrows,
had but an indirect participation in them. Just
when he was most lonely and desolate at the
close of the fatal year he had written to Coleridge : "I can only converse with you by letter
and with the dead in their books. My sister,
indeed, is all I can wish in a companion ; but
our spirits are alike poorly, our reading and
knowledge from the self-same sources, our communication with the scenes of the world alike
narrow. Never having kept separate company
or any 'company' *together*—never having read
separate books and few books *together*, what
knowledge have we to convey to each other ? In
our little range of duties and connections how

few sentiments can take place without friends, with few books, with a taste for religion rather than a strong religious habit! We need some support, some leading-strings to cheer and direct us. You talk very wisely, and be not sparing of *your advice;* continue to remember us and to show us you do remember; we will take as lively an interest in what concerns you and yours. All I can add to your happiness will be sympathy; you can add to mine *more;* you can teach me wisdom."

Quite suddenly, at the beginning of the new year, there came to break this solitude Charles Lloyd, whose poems were to company Lamb's own and Coleridge's in the forthcoming volume: a young man of Quaker family who was living in close fellowship with that group of poets down in Somersetshire, towards whom Lamb's eyes and heart were wistfully turned, as afterwards were to be those of all lovers of literature. How deeply he was moved by this spontaneous seeking for his friendship on Lloyd's part, let a few lines from one of those early poems which, in their earnest simplicity and sincerity, are precious autobiographic fragments, tell:—

> Alone, obscure, without a friend,
> A cheerless, solitary thing,
> Why seeks my Lloyd the stranger out?
> What offering can the stranger bring

Of social scenes, home-bred delights,
That him in aught compensate may
For Stowey's pleasant winter nights,
For loves and friendships far away?
   *   *   *   *   *   *
For this a gleam of random joy
Hath flush'd my unaccustom'd cheek,
And with an o'ercharged, bursting heart
I feel the thanks I cannot speak.
O sweet are all the Muses' lays,
And sweet the charm of matin bird —
'Twas long since these estranged ears
The sweeter voice of friend had heard.

The next was a yet brighter gleam — a fortnight with Coleridge at Nether Stowey and an
introduction to Wordsworth and his sister Dorothy, forerunner of a life-long friendship, in
which Mary was soon to share. The visit took
place in the July of this same year, 1797. The
prospect of it had dangled tantalizingly before
Charles' eyes for a year or more; and now at
last his chiefs at the India House were propi-
tious, and he wrote: "May I, can I, shall I come
so soon? . . . I long, I yearn, with all
the longings of a child do I desire to see you,
to come among you, to see the young philosopher [Hartley, the poet's first child], to thank
Sara for her last year's invitation in person, to
read your tragedy, to read over together our
little book, to breathe fresh air, to revive in me
vivid images of '*salutation scenery*.' There is

a sort of sacrilege in my letting such ideas slip
out of my mind and memory. . . . Here
I will leave off, for I dislike to fill up this paper
(which involves a question so connected with
my heart and soul) with meaner matter, or subjects to me less interesting. I can talk as I
can think — nothing else."

Seldom has fate been kind enough to bring
together, in those years of early manhood when
friendships strike their deepest roots, just the
very men who could give the best help, the
warmest encouragement to each other's genius,
whilst they were girding themselves for that
warfare with the ignorance and dullness of the
public which every original man has to wage
for a longer or shorter time. Wordsworth was
twenty - seven, Coleridge twenty - five, Lamb
twenty-two. For Wordsworth was to come the
longest, stiffest battle — fought, however, from
the vantage ground of pecuniary independence,
thanks to his simple, frugal habits and to a few
strokes of good fortune. His aspect in age is
familiar to the readers of this generation, but
less so the Wordsworth of the days when the
Lyrical Ballads were just taking final shape.
There was already a severe, worn pressure of
thought about the temples of his high yet somewhat narrow forehead, and " his eyes were fires,
half smouldering, half burning, inspired, super-

natural, with a fixed acrid gaze," as if he saw
something in objects more than the outward
appearance. "His cheeks were furrowed by
strong purpose and feeling, and there was a
convulsive inclination to laughter about the
mouth, a good deal at variance with the solemn,
stately expression of the rest of his face."
Dressed in a brown fustian jacket and striped
pantaloons, adds Hazlitt, who first saw him a
few months later, he had something of a roll
and lounge in his gait not unlike his own Peter
Bell. He talked freely and naturally, with a
mixture of clear, gushing accents in his voice, a
deep, guttural intonation and a strong tincture
of the northern burr, and when he recited one
of his poems his voice lingered on the ear "like
the roll of spent thunder."

But who could dazzle and win like Coleridge?
Who could travel so far and wide through all
the realms of thought and imagination, and pour
out the riches he brought back in such free, full,
melodious speech, with that spontaneous "utter-
ancy of heart and soul" which was his unique
gift, in a voice whose tones were so sweet, ear
and soul were alike ravished? For him the
fight was not so much with the public, which,
Orpheus that he was, he could so easily have
led captive, as with the flesh — weak health, a
nerveless languor, a feeble will that never could

combine and concentrate his forces for any sustained or methodical effort. Dorothy Wordsworth has described him as he looked in these
days : "At first I thought him very plain — that
is, for about three minutes. He is pale, thin,
has a wide mouth, thick lips, and not very good
teeth, longish, loose-growing, half-curling, rough,
black hair (in both these respects a contrast to
Wordsworth, who had in his youth beautiful
teeth and light brown hair) ; but if you hear
him speak for five minutes you think no more
of them. His eye is large and full and not very
dark, but gray ; such an eye as would receive
from a heavy soul the dullest expression ; but it
speaks every emotion of his animated mind; it
has more of the 'poet's eye in a fine frenzy roll-
ing' than I ever witnessed. He has fine dark
eyebrows and an overhanging forehead." This
was the very year that produced *The Ancient
Mariner*, the first part of *Christabel*, and *Kubla
Khan.*

To Charles Lamb the change from his re-
stricted, overshadowed life in London — all day
at a clerk's desk and in the evening a return to
the Pentonville lodging, with no other inmate
than his poor old father, Sundays and holidays
only spent with his sister, — to such companionship amid such scenes, almost dazed him, like
stepping from a darkened room into the bril-

liant sunshine. Before he went he had written:
"I see nobody. I sit and read, or walk alone and
hear nothing. I am quite lost to conversation
from disuse; and out of the sphere of my little
family (who, I am thankful, are dearer and dearer to me every day), I see no face that brightens
up at my approach. My friends are at a distance.
Worldly hopes are at a low ebb with me, and
unworldly thoughts are unfamiliar to me, though
I occasionally indulge in them. Still, I feel a
calm not unlike content. I fear it is sometimes
more akin to physical stupidity than to a heaven-
flowing serenity and peace. If I come to Stowey,
what conversation can I furnish to compensate
my friend for those stores of knowledge and of
fancy, those delightful treasures of wisdom,
which I know he will open to me? But it is
better to give than to receive; and I was a very
patient hearer and docile scholar in our winter
evening meetings at Mr. May's, was I not, Coleridge? What I have owed to thee my heart
can ne'er forget."

Perhaps his friends, even Coleridge who knew
him so well, realized as little as himself what
was the true mental stature of the "gentle-
hearted" and "wild-eyed boy," as they called
him whose opportunities and experience, save
in the matter of strange calamity, had been so

narrow compared to their own. The keen edge
of his discernment as a critic, quick and piercing as those quick, piercing, restless eyes of his,
they knew and prized, yet could hardly, perhaps, divine that there were qualities in him
which would freight his prose for a long voyage
down the stream of time. But already they
knew that within that small, spare frame, "thin
and wiry as an Arab of the desert," there beat
a heroic heart, fit to meet the stern and painful
exigencies of his lot ; and that his love for his
sister was of the same fibre as conscience — "a
supreme embracer of consequences."

Dorothy Wordsworth was just such a friend
and comrade to the poet as Mary was to
Charles, sharing his passionate devotion to
nature as Mary shared her brother's loves,
whether for men or books, or for the stir and
throng of life in the great city. Alike were
these two women in being, as De Quincey said
of Dorothy, "the truest, most inevitable, and,
at the same time, the quickest and readiest in
sympathy with either joy or sorrow, with laughter or with tears, with the realities of life, or
with the larger realities of the poets." But unlike in temperament ; Dorothy ardent, fiery,
trembling with eager impetuosity that embarrassed her utterance ; Mary gentle, silent or

deliberate in speech. In after-life there was another sad similarity, for Dorothy's reason, too, was in the end over-clouded. Coleridge has described her as she then was : " She is a woman indeed," said he, "in mind, I mean, and in heart ; for her person is such that if you expected to see a pretty woman you would think her ordinary; if you expected to see an ordinary woman you would think her pretty ; but her manners are simple, ardent and impressive. In every motion her innocent soul outbeams so brightly that who saw her would say 'guilt was a thing impossible with her ;' her information various, her eye watchful in minute observation of nature, and her taste a perfect electrometer."

An accident had lamed Coleridge the very morning after Lamb's arrival, so that he was unable to share his friend's walks. He turned his imprisonment to golden account by writing a poem which mirrors for us, as in a still lake, the beauty of the Quantock hills and vales where they were roaming, the scenes amid which these great and happy days of youth and poetry and friendship were passed. It is the very poem in the margin of which, eight and thirty years afterwards, Coleridge on his deathbed wrote down the sum of his love for Charles and Mary Lamb : —

THIS LIME-TREE BOWER MY PRISON.

Well, they are gone, and here must I remain,
This lime-tree bower my prison! I have lost
Beauties and feelings such as would have been
Most sweet to my remembrance even when age
Had dimmed mine eyes to blindness! They, meanwhile,
Friends whom I never more may meet again
On springy heath, along the hill-top edge
Wander in gladness and wind down, perchance,
To that still roaring dell of which I told;
The roaring dell, o'erwooded, narrow, deep,
And only speckled by the mid-day sun;
Where its slim trunk the ash from rock to rock
Flings arching like a bridge; — that branchless ash,
Unsunned and damp, whose few poor yellow leaves
Ne'er tremble in the gale, yet tremble still,
Fanned by the water-fall! and there my friends
Behold the dark green file of long, lank weeds,
That all at once (a most fantastic sight!)
Still nod and drip before the dripping edge
Of the blue clay-stone.
⠀⠀⠀⠀⠀⠀⠀⠀⠀Now my friends emerge
Beneath the wide, wide heaven — and view again
The many-steepled tract magnificent
Of hilly fields and meadows, and the sea,
With some fair bark, perhaps, whose sails light up
The slip of smooth clear blue betwixt two isles
Of purple shadow! Yes! they wander on
In gladness all; but thou, methinks, most glad,
My gentle-hearted Charles! for thou hast pined
And hungered after Nature many a year,
In the great city pent, winning thy way
With sad yet patient soul, through evil and pain
And strange calamity! Ah! slowly sink

Behind the western ridge, thou glorious sun!
Shine in the slant beams of the sinking orb,
Ye purple heath-flowers! richlier burn, ye clouds!
Live in the yellow light, ye distant groves!
And kindle, thou blue ocean! So my friend,
Struck with deep joy, may stand, as I have stood,
Silent with swimming sense; yea, gazing round
On the wide landscape, gaze till all doth seem
Less gross than bodily; and of such hues
As veil the Almighty Spirit, when yet He makes
Spirits perceive His presence.

     *   *   *   *   *   *

On Lamb's return he wrote in the same mod.
est vein as before: —

"I am scarcely yet so reconciled to the loss
of you or so subsided into my wonted uniformi-
ty of feeling as to sit calmly down to think of
you and write. . . . Is the patriot [Thelwall]
come? Are Wordsworth and his sister gone
yet? I was looking out for John Thelwall all
the way from Bridgewater, and had I met him I
think it would have moved me almost to tears.
You will oblige me, too, by sending me my
great-coat, which I left behind in the oblivious
state the mind is thrown into at parting. Is it
not ridiculous that I sometimes envy that great-
coat lingering so cunningly behind! At present I have none; so send it me by a Stowey
wagon if there be such a thing, directing it for
C. L., No. 45 Chapel street, Pentonville, near

London.   But above all, *that inscription* [of
Wordsworth's]. It will recall to me the tones
of all your voices, and with them many a remembered kindness to one who could and can
repay you all only by the silence of a grateful
heart.   I could not talk much while I was with
you, but my silence was not sullenness nor, I
hope, from any bad motive ; but in truth, disuse
has made me awkward at it.   I know I behaved
myself, particularly at Tom Poole's and at
Cruikshank's, most like a sulky child ; but company and converse are strange to me.   It was
kind in you all to endure me as you did.

" Are you and your dear Sara — to me also
very dear because very kind — agreed yet about
the management of little Hartley ? And how go
on the little rogue's teeth ? "

The mention of his address in the foregoing
letter shows that Lamb and his father had already quitted Little Queen street.   It is probable that they did so, indeed, immediately after
the great tragedy ; to escape not only from the
painful associations of the spot, but also from
the cruel curiosity which its terrible notoriety
must have drawn upon them.   The season was
coming round which could not but renew his
and Mary's grief and anguish in the recollection
of that " day of horrors. " " Friday next, Coleridge, " he writes, " is the day (September 22d)

on which my mother died; "and in the letter is inclosed that beautiful and affecting poem beginning : —

> Alas ! how am I changed ?   Where be the tears,
> The sobs, and forced suspensions of the breath,
> And all the dull desertions of the heart,
> With which I hung o'er my dead mother's corse ?
> Where be the blest subsidings of the storm
> Within ?   The sweet resignedness of hope
> Drawn heavenward, and strength of filial love
> In which I bowed me to my Father's will ?
>
> *   *   *   *   *   *

Mary's was a silent grief.   But those few casual pathetic words written years afterwards speak her life-long sorrow, — "my dear mother, who, though you do not know it, is always in my poor head and heart. "   She continued quiet in her lodgings, free from relapse, till toward the end of the year.

On the 10th of December Charles wrote in bad spirits : — "My teasing lot makes me too confused for a clear judgment of things ; too selfish for sympathy. . . . My sister is pretty well, thank God.   We think of you very often. God bless you !   Continue to be my correspondent, and I will strive to fancy that this world is *not* 'all barrenness.' "

But by Christmas Day she was once more in the asylum.   In sad solitude he gave utterance, again in verse form, to his overflowing grief and love : —

I am a widow'd thing now thou art gone!
Now thou art gone, my own familiar friend,
Companion, sister, helpmate, counsellor!
Alas! that honor'd mind whose sweet reproof
And meekest wisdom in times past have smooth'd
The unfilial harshness of my foolish speech,
And made me loving to my parents old.
(Why is this so, ah God! why is this so?)
That honor'd mind becomes a fearful blank,
Her senses lock'd up, and herself kept out
From human sight or converse, while so many
Of the foolish sort are left to roam at large,
Doing all acts of folly and sin and shame?
Thy paths are mystery!
                  Yet I will not think,
Sweet friend, but we shall one day meet and live
In quietness and die so, fearing God.
Or if *not*, and these false suggestions be
A fit of the weak nature, loth to part
With what it loved so long and held so dear;
If thou art to be taken and I left
(More sinning, yet unpunish'd save in thee),
It is the will of God, and we are clay
In the potter's hand; and at the worst are made
From absolute nothing, vessels of disgrace,
Till His most righteous purpose wrought in us,
Our purified spirits find their perfect rest.

To add to these sorrows Coleridge had, for
some time, been growing negligent as a correspondent. So early as April Lamb had written,
after affectionate inquiries for Hartley, "the
minute philosopher," and Hartley's mother:

3

"Coleridge, I am not trifling, nor are these matter-of-fact questions only. You are all very dear and precious to me. Do what you will, Coleridge ; you may hurt and vex me by your silence, but you cannot estrange my heart from you all. I cannot scatter friendships like chuck-farthings, nor let them drop from mine hand like hour-glass sand. I have but two or three people in the world to whom I am more than indifferent, and I can't afford to whistle them off to the winds."

And again, three months after his return from Stowey, he wrote sorrowfully, almost plaintively, remonstrating for Lloyd's sake and his own : —

"You use Lloyd very ill, never writing to him. I tell you again that his is not a mind with which you should play tricks. He deserves more tenderness from you. For myself, I must spoil a little passage of Beaumont and Fletcher's to adapt it to my feelings : —

> I am prouder
> That I was once your friend, tho' now forgot,
> Than to have had another true to me.

If you don't write to me now, as I told Lloyd, I shall get angry and call you hard names — 'Man-chineel'" (alluding to a passage in a poem of Coleridge's, where he compares a false friend to

the treacherous manchineel tree, * which min-
gles its own venom with the rain and poisons
him who rests beneath its shade), "and I don't
know what else. I wish you would send me
my great-coat. The snow and rain season is at
hand and I have but a wretched old coat, once
my father's, to keep 'em off, and that is transi-
tory.

> When time drives flocks from field to fold,
> When ways grow foul and blood gets cold,

I shall remember where I left my coat. Meet
emblem wilt thou be, old Winter, of a friend's
neglect — cold, cold, cold ! "

But this fresh stroke of adversity, sweeping
away the fond hope Charles had begun to cher-
ish that "Mary would never be so ill again,"
roused his friend's sometimes torpid but deep
and enduring affection for him into action.
"You have writ me many kind letters, and I
have answered none of them," says Lamb, on
the 28th of January, 1798. "I don't deserve
your attention. An unnatural indifference has
been creeping on me since my last misfortunes,
or I should have seized the first opening of a
correspondence with you. These last afflic-
tions, Coleridge, have failed to soften and bend

* *Hippomane Nancinella*, one of the *Euphorbiaceæ*, a
native of South America.

my will. They found me unprepared. . . .
I have been very querulous, impatient under
the rod — full of little jealousies and heart-
burnings. I had well-nigh quarreled with
Charles Lloyd ; and for no other reason, I believe, than that the good creature did all he
could to make me happy. The truth is, I
thought he tried to force my mind from its natural and proper bent. He continually wished
me to be from home ; he was drawing me *from*
the consideration of my poor dear Mary's situation rather than assisting me to gain a proper
view of it with religious consolations. I wanted
to be left to the tendency of my own mind, in a
solitary state which in times past, I knew, had
led to quietness and a patient bearing of the
yoke. He was hurt that I was not more constantly with him ; but he was living with White
(Jem White, an old school-fellow, author of
Falstaff's Letters), a man to whom I had never
been accustomed to impart my *dearest feelings*,
though, from long habits of friendliness and
many a social and good quality, I loved him
very much. I met company there sometimes,
indiscriminate company. Any society almost,
when I am in affliction, is sorely painful to me.
I seem to breathe more freely, to think more
collectedly, to feel more properly and calmly
when alone. All these things the good creat-

ure did with the kindest intentions in the
world, but they produced in me nothing but
screness and discontent. I became, as he complained, 'jaundiced' towards him, . . . but
he has forgiven me; and his smile, I hope, will
draw all such humors from me. I am recovering, God be praised for it, a healthiness of
mind, something like calmness; but I want
more religion. . . . Mary is recovering; but
I see no opening yet of a situation for her.
Your invitation went to my very heart; but you
have a power of exciting interest, of leading all
hearts captive, too forcible to admit of Mary's
being with you. I consider her as perpetually
on the brink of madness. I think you would
almost make her dance within an inch of the
precipice: she must be with duller fancies and
cooler intellects. I know a young man of this
description, who has suited her these twenty
years, and may live to do so still, if we are one
day restored to each other."

But the clouds gathered up again between the
friends, generated partly by a kind of intellectual arrogance whereof Coleridge afterwards
accused himself (he was often but too self-de-
preciatory in after-life), which, in spite of Lamb's
generous and unbounded admiration for his
friend, did at last both irritate and hurt him;
still more by the influence of Lloyd, who, him-

self slighted, as he fancied, and full of a morbid sensitiveness "bordering on derangement," sometimes, indeed, overleaping that border, worked upon Lamb's soreness of feeling till a brief estrangement ensued. Lamb had not yet learned to be on his guard with Lloyd. Years afterwards he wrote of him to Coleridge : "He is a sad tattler ; but this is under the rose. Twenty years ago he estranged one friend from me quite, whom I have been regretting, but never could regain since. He almost alienated you also from me or me from you, I don't know which : but that breach is closed. The 'dreary sea' is filled up. He has lately been at work 'telling again,' as they call it, a most gratuitous piece of mischief, and has caused a coolness betwixt me and (not a friend but) an intimate acquaintance. I suspect, also, he saps Manning's faith in me, who am to Manning more than an acquaintance."

The breach was closed, indeed, almost as soon as opened. But Coleridge went away to Germany for fourteen months and the correspondence was meanwhile suspended. When it was resumed Lamb was, in some respects, an altered man ; he was passing from youth to maturity, enlarging the circle of his acquaintance and entering on more or less continuous literary work ; whilst, on the other hand, the weaknesses which accompanied the splendid endowments of his friend were becoming but too plainly apparent; and though they never for a moment lessened Lamb's affection, nay, with his fine humanity seemed to give rather an added tenderness to it, there was inevitably a less deferential, a more humorous and playful tone on his side in their intercourse. "Bless you, old sophist, who, next to human nature, taught me all the corruption I was capable of knowing," says he to the poet-philosopher by and by. And the weak side of his friend's style, too, received an occasional sly thrust; as, for instance, when on forwarding him some books he writes in 1800: "I detained *Statius* wilfully, out of a reverent regard to your style. *Statius*, they tell me, is turgid."

CHAPTER IV.

Death of the Father. — Mary comes Home to live. — A
Removal. — First Verses. — A Literary Tea-party. —
Another move. — Friends increase.

1799–1800. — Æt. 35–36.

THE feeble flame of life in Lamb's father flick-
ered on for two years and a half after his wife's
death. He was laid to rest at last beside her
and his sister Hetty in the churchyard of St.
Andrew's, Holborn (now swept away in the
building of the Holborn Viaduct), on the 13th
of April, 1799, and Mary came home once more.
There is no mention of either fact in Lamb's
letters; for Coleridge was away in Germany;
and with Southey, who was almost the sole correspondent of this year, the tie was purely intellectual and never even in that kind a close
one. A significant allusion to Mary there is,
however, in a letter to him dated May 20 : —
"Mary was never in better health or spirits
than now." But neither the happiness of sharing Charles' home again nor anything else could
save her from the constant recurrence of her
malady ; nor, in these early days, from the pain-

ful notoriety of what had befallen her ; and they were soon regarded as unwelcome inmates in the Chapel street lodgings. Early in 1800 he tells Coleridge : "Soon after I wrote to you last an offer was made me by Gutch (you must remember him at Christ's) to come and lodge with him at his house in Southampton Buildings, Chancery Lane. This was a very comfortable offer to me, the rooms being at a reasonable rent and including the use of an old servant, besides being infinitely preferable to ordinary lodgings *in our case*, as you must perceive. As Gutch knew all our story and the perpetual liability to a recurrence in my sister's disorder, probably to the end of her life, I certainly think the offer very generous and very friendly. I have got three rooms (including servant) under £34 a year. Here I soon found myself at home, and here, in six weeks after, Mary was well enough to join me. So we are once more settled. I am afraid we are not placed out of the reach of future interruptions ; but I am determined to take what snatches of pleasure we can, between the acts of our distressful drama. I have passed two days at Oxford, on a visit, which I have long put off, to Gutch's family. The sight of the Bodleian Library, and, above all, a fine bust of Bishop Taylor at All Souls', were particularly gratifying to me. Unluckily it was not a fam-

ily where I could take Mary with me, and I
am afraid there is something of dishonesty in
any pleasure I take without *her*. She never
goes anywhere." And to Manning: "It is a
great object for me to live in town." [Penton-
ville then too much of a gossiping country sub-
urb!] "We can be nowhere private except in
the midst of London."

By the summer Mary was not only quite well,
but making a first essay in verse — the theme a
playful mockery of her brother's boyish love for
a pictured beauty at Blakesware described in
his essay, — "that beauty with the cool, blue,
pastoral drapery and a lamb, that hung next the
great bay window, with the bright yellow
H——shire hair, and eye of watchet hue — so
like my Alice! I am persuaded she was a true
Elia — Mildred Elia, I take it. From her and
from my passion for her — for I first learned
love from a picture — Bridget took the hint of
those pretty whimsical lines which thou mayest
see if haply thou hast never seen them, reader,
in the margin. But my Mildred grew not old
like the imaginary Helen."

With brotherly pride he sends them to Coleridge: "How do you like this little epigram?
It is not my writing, nor had I any finger in it.
If you concur with me in thinking it very elegant and very original, I shall be tempted to

name the author to you.   I will just hint that it
is almost or quite a first attempt" : —

HELEN.

High-born Helen, round your dwelling
   These twenty years I've paced in vain ;
Haughty beauty, thy lover's duty
   Hath been to glory in his pain.

High-born Helen, proudly telling
   Stories of thy cold disdain ;
I starve, I die, now you comply,
   And I no longer can complain.

These twenty years I've lived on tears,
   Dwelling forever on a frown ;
On sighs I've fed, your scorn my bread ;
   I perish, now you kind are grown.

Can I who loved my beloved,
   But for the scorn "was in her eye " —
Can I be moved for my beloved,
   When she "returns me sigh for sigh ? "

In stately pride, by my bed-side
   High-born Helen's portrait 's hung ;
Deaf to my praise, my mournful lays
   Are nightly to the portrait sung.

So that I weep, nor ever sleep,
   Complaining all night long to her.
Helen grown old, no longer cold,
   Said, " You to all men I prefer."

Lamb inserted this and another by Mary, a serious and tender little poem, the *Dialogue between a Mother and Child*, beginning:—

> O lady, lay your costly robes aside;
> No longer may you glory in your pride,—

in the first collected edition of his works.

Mary now began also to go out with her brother, and the last record of this year in the Coleridge correspondence discloses them at a literary tea-party, not in the character of lions, but only as friends of a lion — Coleridge — who had already become, in his frequent visits to town, the prey of some third-rate admiring literary ladies, notably of a certain Miss Wesley (niece of John Wesley) and of her friend, Miss Benger, authoress of a *Life of Tobin*, etc.

"You blame us for giving your direction to Miss Wesley," says the letter; "the woman has been ten times after us about it and we gave it her at last, under the idea that no further harm would ensue, but that she would *once* write to you, and you would bite your lips and forget to answer it, and so it would end. You read us a dismal homily upon 'Realities.' We know quite as well as you do what are shadows and what are realities. You, for instance, when you are over your fourth or fifth jorum, chirping about old school occurrences, are the best of realities.

Shadows are cold, thin things that have no
warmth or grasp in them. Miss Wesley and
her friend, and a tribe of authoresses that come
after you here daily, and, in defect of you, hive
and cluster upon us, are the shadows. You en-
couraged that mopsey Miss Wesley to dance
after you in the hope of having her nonsense
put into a nonsensical anthology. We have
pretty well shaken her off by that simple expedient of referring her to you, but there are
more burs in the wind. I came home t' other
day from business, hungry as a hunter, to dinner, with nothing, I am sure, of the author but
hunger about me; and whom found I closeted
with Mary but a friend of this Miss Wesley,
one Miss Benjay or Benje. . . . I just came in
time enough, I believe, luckily to prevent them
from exchanging vows of eternal friendship. It
seems she is one of your authoresses that you
first foster and then upbraid us with. But I
forgive you. 'The rogue has given me potions
to make me love him.' Well, go she would not
nor step a step over our threshold till we had
promised to come to drink tea with her next
night. I had never seen her before and could
not tell who the devil it was that was so familiar. We went, however, not to be impolite.
Her lodgings are up two pair of stairs in East
street. Tea and coffee and macaroons — a kind

of cake — much love. We sat down. Presently
Miss Benjay broke the silence by declaring herself quite of a different opinion from *D'Israeli*,
who supposes the differences of human intellect
to be the mere effect of organization. She
begged to know my opinion. I attempted
to carry it off with a pun upon organ, but
that went off very flat. She immediately con-
ceived a very low opinion of my metaphysics;
and turning round to Mary, put some question
to her in French, possibly having heard that
neither Mary nor I understood French. The
explanation that took place occasioned some
embarrassment and much wondering. She then
fell into an insulting conversation about the
comparative genius and merits of all modern
languages, and concluded with asserting that
the Saxon was esteemed the purest dialect in
Germany. From thence she passed into the
subject of poetry, where I, who had hitherto sat
mute and a hearer only, humbly hoped I might
now put in a word to some advantage, seeing
that it was my own trade in a manner. But I
was stopped by a round assertion that no good
poetry had appeared since Dr. Johnson's time.
It seems the doctor has suppressed many hopeful geniuses that way, by the severity of his
critical strictures in his *Lives of the Poets*. I
here ventured to question the fact and was be-

ginning to appeal to *names*, but I was assured
'it was certainly the case.' Then we discussed
Miss More's [Hannah] book on education, which
I had never read. It seems Dr. Gregory, another of Miss Benjay's friends, had found fault
with one of Miss More's metaphors. Miss More
has been at some pains to vindicate herself, in
the opinion of Miss Benjay not without success.
It seems the doctor is invariably against the
use of broken or mixed metaphor, which he
reprobates, against the authority of Shakespeare himself. We next discussed the question
whether Pope was a poet. I find Dr. Gregory is
of opinion he was not, though Miss Seward
does not at all concur with him in this. We
then sat upon the comparative merits of the
ten translations of Pizarro, and Miss Benjay or
Benje advised Mary to take two of them home
(she thought it might afford her some pleasure
to compare them *verbatim*), which we declined.
It being now nine o'clock, wine and macaroons
were again served round, and we parted with a
promise to go again next week and meet the
Miss Porters, who, it seems, have heard much
of Mr. Coleridge and wish to see *us* because
we are *his* friends. I have been preparing for
the occasion. I crowd cotton in my ears. I
read all the reviews and magazines of the past
month against the dreadful meeting, and I hope

by these means to cut a tolerable second-rate figure.

" . . . . Take no thought about your proof-sheets ; they shall be done as if Woodfall himself did them.   Pray send us word of Mrs. Coleridge and little David Hartley, your little reality.   Farewell, dear Substance.   Take no umbrage at anything I have written.

" I am, and will be,

" Yours ever in sober sadness,

" Land of Shadows,   C. LAMB.   *Umbra.*

" Shadow month, 16th or 17th, 1800.

" Write your German as plain as sunshine, for that must correct itself.   You know I am *homo unius linguæ :* in English — illiterate, a dunce, a ninny. "

Mr. Gutch seems to have soon repented him of his friendly deed : —

" I am going to change my lodgings, having received a hint that it would be agreeable at Our Lady's next feast, " writes Lamb to Manning.   " I have partly fixed upon most delectable rooms which look out (when you stand a-tiptoe) over the Thames and Surrey hills.   .   .   . My bed faces the river, so as by perking up on my haunches and supporting my carcass with my elbows, without much wrying my neck, I can see the white sails glide by the bottom of the King's Bench Walk as I lie in my bed,   .   .

casement windows with small panes to look more like a cottage. . . . There I shall have all the privacy of a house without the encumbrance, and shall be able to lock my friends out as often as I desire to hold free converse with my immortal mind, for my present lodgings resemble a minister's levée, I have so increased my acquaintance (as they call 'em) since I have resided in town. Like the country mouse that had tasted a little of urban manners, I long to be nibbling my own cheese by my dear self, without mouse-traps and time-traps."

These rooms were at No. 16 Mitre Court Buildings, and here Lamb and his sister lived for nine years. But far from "nibbling his own cheese" by himself, there for nine years he and Mary gathered round their hearth and homely, hospitable supper-table, with its bread and cheese in these early days, and by and by its round of beef or "winter hand of pork," an ever-lengthened succession of friends, cronies and acquaintances. There came Manning, with his "fine, skeptical, dogmatical face;" and George Dyer, with his head full of innutritious learning and his heart of the milk of kindness. And Godwin, the man of strange contrasts, a bold thinker, yet ignorant as a child of human nature and weakly vain; with such a "noisy fame," for a time, as if he were "Briareus Cen-

timanus or a Tityus tall enough to pull Jupiter
from his heavens," and then soon forgotten, or
remembered only to be denounced; for a year
the loving husband of one of the sweetest and
noblest of women, and after her death led captive by the coarse flatteries and vulgar pretensions of one of the commonest. "Is it possible
that I behold the immortal Godwin?" said,
from a neighboring balcony, she who in a few
months became his second wife, and in a few
more had alienated some of his oldest friends
and earned the cordial dislike of all, even of
Lamb. "I will be buried with this inscription
over me: 'Here lies C. L., the woman-hater;'
I mean that hated one woman; for the rest,
God bless 'em," was his whimsical way of vent-
ing his feelings towards her; and Shelley experienced the like, though he expressed them less
pungently. Then there was Holcroft, who had
fought his way up from grimmest poverty, misery and ignorance to the position of an accomplished literary man; and fine old Captain Burney, who had been taught his accidence by
Eugene Aram and had sailed round the world
with Captain Cook; and his son, "noisy Martin" with the "spotless soul," for forty years,
boy and man, Mary's favorite; and Phillips, of
the Marines, who was with Captain Cook at his
death and shot the savage that killed him; and

Rickman, "the finest fellow to drop in a'
nights," Southey's great friend, though he
"never read his poetry," as Lamb tells ; staunch
Crabb Robinson ; Fanny Kelly, with her
"divine, plain face," who died but the other
day at the age of ninety-odd ; and Mr. Dawe,
R. A., a figure of nature's own purest comedy.
All these and many more frequented the home
of Charles and Mary Lamb in these years, and
live in their letters.

CHAPTER V.

Personal Appearance and Manners. — Health.— Influence
of Mary's Illness upon her Brother.

No description of Mary Lamb's person in youth
is to be found; but hers was a kind of face
which Time treats gently, adding with one hand
while he takes away with the other; compen-
sating by deepened traces of thought and kind-
liness and loss of youthful freshness. Like her
brother, her features were well formed. "Her
face was pale and somewhat square, very placid,
with gray, intelligent eyes," says Procter, who
first saw her when she was about fifty-three.
"Eyes brown, soft and penetrating," says another friend, Miss Cowden-Clarke, confirming
the observation that it is difficult to judge of
the color of expressive eyes. She, too, lays
stress upon the strong resemblance to Charles
and especially on a smile like his, "winning in
the extreme." De Quincey speaks of her as
"that Madonna-like lady."

The only original portrait of her in existence,
I believe, is that by the late Mr. Cary (son of
Lamb's old friend), now in the possession of

Mr. Edward Hughes, and engraved in the *Memoir* of Lamb, by Barry Cornwall; also in *Scribner's Magazine* for March, 1881, where it is accompanied by a letter from Mr. Cary, which states that it was painted in 1834, when Mary was seventy. She stands a little behind her brother, resting one hand on him and one on the back of his chair. There is a characteristic sweetness in her attitude and the countenance is full of goodness and intelligence; whilst the finer modeling of Charles' features and the intellectual beauty of his head are rendered with considerable success, — Crabb Robinson's strictures notwithstanding, who, it appears, saw not the original, but a poor copy of the figure of Charles. It was from Cary's picture that Mr. Armitage, R. A., executed the portraits of the Lambs in the large fresco on the walls of University College Hall. Among its many groups (of which Crabb Robinson, who commissioned the fresco, is the central figure), that containing the Lambs includes also Wordsworth, Coleridge, Blake and Southey. By an unfortunate clause in the deed of gift the fresco, which is painted in monochrome, is forbidden to be cleaned, even with bread-crumb; it is therefore already very dingy.

In stature Mary was under the middle size and her bodily frame was strong. She could walk fifteen miles with ease; her brother speaks of their having walked thirty miles together, and, even at sixty years of age, she was capable of twelve miles "most days." Regardless of weather, too, as Leigh Hunt pleasantly tells in his *Familiar Epistle in Verse* to Lamb:—

You'll guess why I can't see the snow-covered streets,
Without thinking of you and your visiting feats,
When you call to remembrance how you and one more,
When I wanted it most, used to knock at my door;
For when the sad winds told us rain would come down,
Or when snow upon snow fairly clogg'd up the town,
And dun-yellow fogs brooded over its white,
So that scarcely a being was seen towards night,
Then — then said the lady yclept near and dear:
Now, mind what I tell you — the Lambs will be here.
So I poked up the flame, and she got out the tea,
And down we both sat as prepared as could be;
And then, sure as fate came the knock of you two,
Then the lanthorn, the laugh, and the "Well, how
        d' ye do ? "

Mary's manners were easy, quiet, unpretending; to her brother gentle and tender always, says Mrs. Cowden Clarke. She had often an upward look of peculiar meaning when directed towards him, as though to give him an assurance that all was well with her; and a way of repeating his words assentingly when he spoke to her. "He once said, with his peculiar mode of tenderness beneath blunt, abrupt speech,

'You must die first, Mary.' She nodded with
her little quiet nod and sweet smile, 'Yes, I
must die first, Charles.' " When they were in
company together her eyes followed him everywhere ; and even when he was talking at the
other end of the room she would supply some
word he wanted. Her voice was soft and per-
suasive, with at times a certain catch, a kind of
emotional stress in breathing, which gave a
charm to her reading of poetry and a capti-
vating earnestness to her mode of speech when
addressing those she liked. It was a slight
check that had an eager, yearning effect in her
voice, creating a softened resemblance to her
brother's stammer — that "pleasant little stammer," as Barry Cornwall called it, "just enough to
prevent his making speeches ; just enough to
make you listen eagerly for his words." Like him,
too, she took snuff. "She had a small, white,
delicately-formed hand ; and as it hovered above
the tortoise-shell snuff-box, the act seemed yet
another link of association between the brother
and sister as they sat together over their favorite books."

Mary's dress was always plain and neat ; not
changing much with changing fashions ; yet
with no unfeminine affectation of complete indifference. "I do dearly love worked muslin,"
says she in one of her letters, and the "Man-

ning silks" were worn with no little satisfaction. As she advanced in years she usually
wore black stuff or silk; or on great occasions
a "dove-colored silk, with a kerchief of snow-
white muslin folded across her bosom," with a
cap of the kind in fashion in her youth, a deep-
frilled border and a bow on the top.

Mary's severe nurture, though undoubtedly it
bore with too heavy a strain on her physical
and mental constitution, fitted her morally and
practically for the task which she and her
brother fulfilled to admiration — that of making
an income, which for two-thirds of their joint
lives could not have exceeded two or three hun-
dreds a year, suffice for the heavy expense of
her yearly illness, for an open-handed hospitality and for the wherewithal to help a friend
in need, not to speak of their extensive acquaintance among "the great race of borrowers."
He was, says De Quincey, "*princely* — nothing
short of that in his beneficence. . . . Never
any one have I known in this world upon whom
for bounty, for indulgence and forgiveness, for
charitable construction of doubtful or mixed
actions, and for regal munificence, you might
have thrown yourself with so absolute a reli-
ance as upon this comparatively poor Charles
Lamb." There was a certain old-world fashion
in Mary's speech corresponding to her appear-

ance, which was quaint and pleasant ; "yet she was oftener a listener than a speaker, and beneath her sparing talk and retiring manner few would have suspected the ample information and large intelligence that lay concealed."

But for her portrait sweetly touched in with subtle, tender strokes, such as he who knew and loved her best could alone give, we must turn to Elia's *Mackery End :* — " . . . I have obligations to Bridget extending beyond the period of memory. We house together, old bachelor and maid, in a sort of double singleness, with such tolerable comfort, upon the whole, that I, for one, find in myself no sort of disposition to go out upon the mountains, with the rash king's offspring, to bewail my celibacy. We agree pretty well in our tastes and habits, yet so as ' with a difference.' We are generally in harmony, with occasional bickerings, as it should be among near relations. Our sympathies are rather understood than expressed ; and once, upon my dissembling a tone in my voice more kind than ordinary, my cousin burst into tears and complained that I was altered. We are both great readers, in different directions. While I am hanging over, for the thousandth time, some passage in old Burton, or one of his strange contemporaries, she is abstracted in some modern tale or adventure,

whereof our common reading-table is daily fed
with assiduously fresh supplies.   Narrative
teases me.   I have little concern in the progress of events.   She must have a story — well,
ill or indifferently told — so there be life stirring in it and plenty of good or evil accidents.
The fluctuations of fortune in fiction, and almost
in real life, have ceased to interest or operate
but dully upon me.   Out-of-the-way humors and
opinions — heads with some diverting twist in
them — the oddities of authorship, please me
most. • My cousin has a native disrelish of anything that sounds odd or bizarre.   Nothing goes
down with her that is quaint, irregular or out of
the road of common sympathy.   She holds nature
more clever.   .   .   . We are both of us inclined
to be a little too positive ; and I have observed
the result of our disputes to be almost uniformly this : that in matters of fact, dates and circumstances, it turns out that I was in the right and
my cousin in the wrong.   But where we have
differed upon moral points, upon something
proper to be done or let alone, whatever heat
of opposition or steadiness of conviction I set
out with, I am sure always, in the long run, to
be brought over to her way of thinking.   I
must touch upon foibles of my kinswoman with
a gentle hand, for Bridget does not like to be
told of her faults.   She hath an awkward trick

(to say no worse of it) of reading in company ;
at which times she will answer *yes* or *no* to a
question without fully understanding its purport, which is provoking and derogatory in the
highest degree to the dignity of the putter of
the said question. Her presence of mind is
equal to the most pressing trials of life, but will
sometimes desert her upon trifling occasions.
When the purpose requires it, and is a thing of
moment, she can speak to it greatly ; but in
matters which are not stuff of the conscience
she hath been known sometimes to let slip a
word less seasonably. . .

"In seasons of distress she is the truest comforter, but in the teasing accidents and minor
perplexities which do not call out the *will* to
meet them, she sometimes maketh matters
worse by an excess of participation. If she
does not always divide your trouble, upon the
pleasanter occasions of life she is sure always
to treble your satisfaction. She is excellent to
be at a play with, or upon a visit ; but best when
she goes a journey with you."

"Little could any one, observing Miss Lamb
in the habitual serenity of her demeanor,"
writes Talfourd, "guess the calamity in which
she had partaken or the malady which frightfully checkered her life. From Mr. Lloyd, who,
although saddened by impending delusion, was

always found accurate in his recollection of long-
past events and conversations, I learned that
she had described herself, on her recovery from
the fatal attack, as having experienced while it
was subsiding such a conviction that she was
absolved in Heaven from all taint of the deed
in which she had been the agent — such an assurance that it was a dispensation of Providence
for good, though so terrible — such a sense that
her mother knew her entire innocence and shed
down blessings upon her, as though she had
seen the reconcilement in solemn vision — that
she was not sorely afflicted by the recollection.
It was as if the old Greek notion of the necessity for the unconscious shedder of blood, else
polluted though guiltless, to pass through a religious purification, had in her case been happily accomplished; so that not only was she
without remorse, but without other sorrow than
attends on the death of an infirm parent in a
good old age.   She never shrank from alluding
to her mother when any topic connected with
her own youth made such a reference, in ordinary respects, natural; but spoke of her as
though no fearful remembrance was associated
with the image ; so that some of her most intimate friends who knew of the disaster believed
that she had never become aware of her own
share in its horrors.   It is still more singular

that in the wanderings of her insanity, amidst all the vast throngs of imagery she presented of her early days, this picture never recurred, or, if it ever did, not associated with shapes of terror."

Perhaps this was not so surprising as at first sight it appears; for the deed was done in a state of frenzy, in which the brain could no more have received a definite impression of the scene than waves lashed by storm can reflect an image. Her knowledge of the facts was never colored by consciousness, but came to her from without, "as a tale that is told." The statement, also, that Mary could always speak calmly of her mother, seems to require some qualification. Emma Isola, Lamb's adopted daughter, afterwards Mrs. Moxon, once asked her, ignorant of the facts, why she never spoke of her mother, and was answered only with a cry of distress; probably the question, coming abruptly and from a child, confronted her in a new, sudden and peculiarly painful way with the tragedy of her youth.

"Miss Lamb would have been remarkable for the sweetness of her disposition, the clearness of her understanding, and the gentle wisdom of all her acts and words," continues Talfourd, "even if these qualities had not been presented in marvelous contrast with the distractions under which she suffered for weeks, latter-

ly for months in every year. There was no tinge
of insanity discernible in her manner to the
most observant eye : not even in those distressful periods when the premonitory symptoms
had apprised her of its approach, and she was
making preparations for seclusion." This, too,
must be taken with some qualification. In a
letter from Coleridge to Matilda Betham he
mentions that Mary had been to call on the
Godwins, "and that her manner of conversation
had greatly alarmed them (dear, excellent creature! such is the restraining power of her love
for Charles Lamb over her mind, that he is always the last person in whose presence any
alienation of her understanding betrays itself);
that she talked far more and with more agitation
concerning me than about G. Burnet [the too
abrupt mention of whose death had upset her;
he was an old friend and one of the original
Pantisocratic group], and told Mrs. Godwin that
she herself had written to William Wordsworth,
exhorting him to come to town immediately,
for that my mind was seriously unhinged." To
resume. "Her character," wrote Talfourd, "in
all its essential sweetness, was like her brother's ;
while, by a temper more placid, a spirit of enjoyment more serene, she was enabled to guide,
to counsel, to cheer him and to protect him on
the verge of the mysterious calamity from the

depths of which she rose so often unruffled to his side. To a friend in any difficulty she was the most comfortable of advisers, the wisest of consolers. Hazlitt used to say that he never met with a woman who could reason and had met with only one thoroughly reasonable — the sole exception being Mary Lamb. She did not wish, however, to be made an exception, to the general disparagement of her sex; for in all her thoughts and feelings she was most womanly — keeping under even undue subordination to her notion of a woman's province, an intellect of rare excellence which flashed out when the restraints of gentle habit and humble manner were withdrawn by the terrible force of disease. Though her conversation in sanity was never marked by smartness or repartee, seldom rising beyond that of a sensible, quiet gentlewoman, appreciating and enjoying the talents of her friends, it was otherwise in her madness. Lamb, in his letter to Miss Fryer announcing his determination to be entirely with her, speaks of her pouring out memories of all the events and persons of her younger days; but he does not mention, what I am able from repeated experiences to add, that her ramblings often sparkled with brilliant description and shattered beauty. She would fancy herself in the days of Queen Anne or George the First; and describe the brocaded dames and courtly manners as though she had been bred among them, in the best style of the old comedy. It was all broken and disjointed, so that the hearer could remember little of her discourse; but the fragments were like the jeweled speeches of Congreve, only shaken from their settings. There was sometimes even a vein of crazy logic running through them, associating things essentially most dissimilar, but connecting them by a verbal association in strange order. As a mere physical instance of deranged intellect, her condition was, I believe, extraordinary; it was as if the finest elements of the mind had been shaken into fantastic combinations, like those of a kaleidoscope."

The immediate cause of her attacks would generally seem to have been excitement or overfatigue, causing, in the first instance, loss of sleep, a feverish restlessness, and ending in the complete overthrow of reason. "Her relapses," says Procter, "were not dependent on the seasons; they came in hot weather and with the freezing winters. The only remedy seems to have been extreme quiet when any slight sympton of uneasiness was apparent. If any exciting talk occurred Charles had to dismiss his friend with a whisper. If any stupor or extraordinary silence was observed, then he had to rouse her instantly. He has been seen to take the kettle from the fire and place it for a moment on her head-dress, in order to startle her into recollection." Once the sudden announcement of the marriage of a young friend, whose welfare she had at heart, restored her in a moment, after a protracted illness, "as if by an electric stroke, to the entire possession of her senses." But if no precautions availed to remove the premonitory symptom, then would Mary "as gently as possible prepare her brother for the duty he must perform ; and thus, unless he could stave off the terrible separation till Sunday, oblige him to ask leave of absence from the office, as if for a day's pleasure—a bitter mockery ! On one occasion Mr. Charles Lloyd met them slowly pacing together a little foot-path in Hoxton fields, both weeping bitterly, and found, on joining them, that they were taking their solemn way to the accustomed asylum." Holiday trips were almost always followed by a seizure ; and never did Mary set out on one but with her own hands she packed a straight waist-coat.

The attacks were commonly followed by a period of extreme depression, a sense of being shattered, and by a painful loss of self-reliance. These were but temporary states, however. Mary's habitual frame of mind was, as Talfourd says, serene and capable of placid enjoyment.

4

In her letters to Sara Stoddart there are some affecting and probably unique disclosures of how one who is suffering from madness feels; and what, taught by her own experience, Mary regarded as the most important points in the management of the insane. In reference to her friend's mother, who was thus afflicted, she writes:—

"Do not, I conjure you, let her unhappy malady afflict you too deeply. I speak *from experience* and from the opportunity I have had of much observation in such cases, that insane people, in the fancies they take into their heads, do not feel as one in a sane state of mind does under the real evil of poverty, the perception of having done wrong, or of any such thing that runs in their heads.

"Think as little as you can, and let your whole care be to be certain that she is treated with *tenderness*. I lay a stress upon this because it is a thing of which people in her state are uncommonly susceptible, and which hardly any one is at all aware of; a hired nurse *never*, even though in all other respects they are good kind of people. I do not think your own presence necessary, unless she *takes to you very much*, except for the purpose of seeing with your own eyes that she is very kindly treated.

"I do long to see you! God bless and comfort you."

And again a few weeks later : —

"After a very feverish night I writ a letter to you and I have been distressed about it ever since. That which gives me most concern is the way in which I talked about your mother's illness, and which I have since feared you might construe into my having a doubt of your showing her proper attention without my impertinent interference. God knows, nothing of this kind was ever in my thoughts, but I have entered very deeply into your affliction with regard to your mother; and while I was writing, the many poor souls in the kind of desponding way she is, whom I have seen, came fresh into my mind, and all the mismanagement with which I have seen them treated was strong in my mind, and I wrote under a forcible impulse which I could not at the time resist, but I have fretted so much about it since, that I think it is the last time I will ever let my pen run away with me.

"Your kind heart will, I know, even if you have been a little displeased, forgive me when I assure you my spirits have been so much hurt by my last illness, that at times I hardly know what I do. I do not mean to alarm you about myself or to plead an excuse ; but I am very much otherwise than you have always known me. I do not think any one perceives me altered, but I have lost all self-confidence in my own actions, and one cause of my low spirits is that I never feel satisfied with anything I do — a perception of not being in a sane state perpetually haunts me. I am ashamed to confess this weakness to you ; which, as I am so sensible of, I ought to strive to conquer. But I tell you that you may excuse any part of my letter that has given offense ; for your not answering it, when you are such a punctual correspondent, has made me very uneasy.

"Write immediately, my dear Sara, but do not notice this letter, nor do not mention anything I said relative to your poor mother. Your handwriting will convince me you are friends with me ; and if Charles, who must see my letter, was to know I had first written foolishly and then fretted about the event of my folly, he would both ways be angry with me.

"I would desire you to direct to me at home, but your hand is so well known to Charles that that would not do. Therefore, take no notice of my megrims till we meet, which I most ardently long to do. An hour spent in your company would be a cordial to my drooping heart.

"Write, I beg, by the return of post ; and as I am very anxious to hear whether you are, as I fear, dissatisfied with me, you shall, if you please, direct my letter to nurse. I do not mean to continue a secret correspondence, but you must oblige me with this one letter. In future I will always show my letters before they go, which will be a proper check upon my wayward pen."

But it was upon her brother that the burthen lay heaviest. It was on his brain that the cruel image of the mother's death-scene was burnt in, and that the grief and loneliness consequent on Mary's ever-recurring attacks pressed sorest.

" His anxiety for her health, even in his most convivial moments, was unceasing. If in company he perceived she looked languid, he would repeatedly ask her, ' Mary, does your head ache ? Don't you feel unwell?' and would be satisfied with none of her gentle assurances that his fears were groundless. He was always fearful of her sensibilities being too deeply engaged, and if in her presence any painful accident or history was discussed, he would turn the conversation with some desperate joke." Miss Betham related to Talfourd that once, when she was speaking to Miss Lamb of her brother, and in her earnestness Mary had laid her hand kindly on the eulogist's shoulder, he came up hastily and interrupted them, saying, "Come, come, we must not talk sentimentally," and took up the conversation in his gayest strain.

The constant anxiety, the forebodings, the unremitting, watchful scrutiny of his sister's state, produced a nervous tension and irritability that pervaded his whole life and manifested themselves in many different ways.

"When she discovers symptoms of approaching illness," he once wrote to Dorothy Wordsworth, "it is not easy to say what is best to do. Being by ourselves is bad and going out is bad. I get so irritable and wretched with fear that I constantly hasten on the disorder. You cannot conceive the misery of such a foresight. I am sure that for the week before she left me I was little better than light-headed. I now am calm, but sadly taken down and flat." Well might he say, "My waking life has much of the confusion, the trouble and obscure perplexity of an ill dream." For he, too, had to wrestle in his own person with the same foe, the same hereditary tendency; though, after one overthrow of reason in his youth, he wrestled successfully. But the frequent allusions in his letters, especially in later years, to attacks of nervous fever, sleeplessness, and depression "black as a smith's beard, Vulcanic, Stygian," show how near to the brink he was sometimes dragged. "You do not know how sore and weak a brain I have, or you would allow for many things which you set down to whim," he wrote to God-

EFFECT UPON HER BROTHER.

win. And again, when there had been some coolness between them : " . . . did the black Hypochondria never gripe *thy* heart till thou hast taken a friend for an enemy ? The foul fiend Flibbertigibbet leads me over four-inched bridges to course my own shadow for a traitor. . . ."

"Yet nervous, tremulous as he seemed," writes Talfourd, "so slight of frame that he looked only fit for the most placid fortune, when the dismal emergencies which checkered his life arose, he acted with as much promptitude and vigor as if he were strung with herculean sinews." "Such fortitude in his manners, and such a ravage of suffering in his countenance did he display," said Coleridge, "as went to the hearts of his friends." It was rather by the violence of the reaction that a keen observer might have estimated the extent of these sufferings ; by that "escape from the pressure of agony, into a fantastic, sometimes almost demoniac mirth, which made Lamb a problem to strangers, while it endeared him thousandfold to those who really knew him."

> The child of impulse ever to appear,
> And yet through duty's path strictly to steer,
> O Lamb, thou art a mystery to me !
> Thou art so prudent, and so mad with wildness —

wrote Charles Lloyd.

Sweet and strong must have been the nature upon which the crush of so severe a destiny produced no soreness, no bitterness, no violence, but only the rebound of a wild, fantastic gaiety. In his writings not only is there an entire absence of the morbid, the querulous; I can find but one expression that breathes of what his sombre experiences were. It is in that most masterly of all his criticisms (unless it be the one on *Lear*), the *Genius and Character of Hogarth*, where, in the sublime description of the Bedlam scene in the *Rake's Progress*, he tells of "the frightful, obstinate laugh of madness." In one apparent way only did the calamity which overshadowed his life exert an influence on his genius. It turned him, as Talfourd finely suggests, "to seek a kindred interest in the sterner stuff of old tragedy—to catastrophes more fearful even than his own—to the aspects of pale passion, to shapes of heroic daring and more heroic suffering, to the agonizing contests of opposing affections and the victories of the soul over calamity and death, which the old English drama discloses, and in the contemplation of which he saw his own suffering nature at once mirrored and exalted." In short, no man ever stood more nobly the test of life-long affliction: "a deep distress had humanized his soul."

Only on one point did the stress of his difficult lot find him vulnerable, one flaw bring to
light — a tendency to counteract his depression
and take the edge off his poignant anxieties by
a too free use of stimulants. The manners of
his day, the custom of producing wine and
strong drinks on every possible occasion, bore
hard on such a craving and fostered a man's
weakness. But Lamb maintained to the end a
good standing fight with the enemy, and, if not
wholly victorious, still less was he wholly de-
feated. So much on account of certain home
anxieties to which Mary's letters to Sara Stoddart make undisguised allusion.

CHAPTER VI.

Visit to Coleridge at Greta Hall. — Wordsworth and his
    Sister in London. — Letters to Miss Stoddart. — Col-
    eridge goes to Malta. — Letter to Dorothy Words-
    worth on the Death of her Brother John.

1802–1805. — Æt. 38–41.

In the summer of 1802, when holiday-time
came round, Charles was siezed with "a strong
desire of visiting remote regions;" and after
some whimsical deliberations his final resolve
was to go with Mary to see Coleridge at the
lakes.

"I set out with Mary to Keswick," he tells
Manning, "without giving any notice to Coleridge [who was now living at Greta Hall, soon
to become Southey's home for the rest of his
life], for my time, being precious, did not admit
of it. We got in in the evening, travelling in a
post-chaise from Penrith, in the midst of a gorgeous sunset which transmuted the mountains
into all colors, purple, etc. We thought we had
got into fairy-land; but that went off (and it
never came again while we stayed, and we had

no more fine sunsets), and we entered Coleridge's comfortable study just in the dusk, when the mountains were all dark with clouds upon their heads. Such an impression I never received from objects of sight before nor do I suppose I ever can again. Glorious creatures, fine old fellows, Skiddaw, etc., I shall never forget ye — how ye lay about that night like an intrenchment; gone to bed, as it seemed, for the night, but promising that ye were to be seen in the morning. Coleridge had got a blazing fire in his study, which is a large, antique, ill-shaped room with an old-fashioned organ, never played upon, big enough for a church; shelves of scattered folios, an Æolian harp and an old sofa half-bed, etc. And all looking out upon the last fading view of Skiddaw and his broad-breasted brethren. What a night!"

The poet had now a second son, or rather a third (for the second had died in infancy), Derwent, a fine, bright, fair, broad-chested little fellow not quite two years old, with whom Charles and Mary were delighted. A merry sprite he was, in a yellow frock which obtained for him the nickname of Stumpy Canary, who loved to race from kitchen to parlor and from parlor to kitchen, just putting in his head at the door with a rougish smile to catch notice, then off again, shaking his little sides with

laughter. He fairly won their hearts, and long
after figures in their letters as Pi-pos Pot-pos,
his own way of pronouncing striped opossum
and spotted opossum, which he would point out
triumphantly in his picture-book. Hartley, now
six, was a prematurely grave and thoughtful
child who had already, as a curious anecdote
told by Crabb Robinson shows, begun to take
surprising plunges into "the metaphysic well
without a bottom;" for once, when asked something about himself and called by name, he
said, "Which Hartley?" "Why, is there
more than one Hartley?" "Yes, there's a
deal of Hartleys; there's Picture Hartley [Haz-
litt had painted his portrait] and Shadow Hartley, and there's Echo Hartley and there's Catch-
me-fast Hartley," seizing his own arm with the
other hand; thereby showing, said his father,
that "he had begun to reflect on what Kant
calls the great and inexplicable mystery that
man should be both his own subject and object,
and that these should yet be one!"

Three delightful weeks they stayed. "So
we have seen," continues Lamb to Manning,
"Keswick, Grasmere, Ambleside, Ulswater
(where the Clarksons live), and a place at the
other end of Ulswater; I forget the name [Pat-
terdale] to which we travelled on a very sultry
day, over the middle of Helvellyn. We have

clambered up to the top of Skiddaw and I have
waded up the bed of Lodore. Mary was excess-
ively tired when she got about half-way up
Skiddaw, but we came to a cold rill (than which
nothing can be imagined more cold, running
over cold stones), and, with the reinforcement
of a draught of cold water, she surmounted it
most manfully. Oh, its fine black head! and
the bleak air atop of it, with the prospect of
mountains all about and about making you giddy ; and then Scotland afar off and the border
countries so famous in song and ballad ! It was
a day that will stand out like a mountain, I am
sure, in my life."

Wordsworth was away at Calais, but the
Lambs stayed a day or so in his cottage with
the Clarksons (he of slavery abolition fame and
she "one of the friendliest, comfortablest women
we know, who made the little stay one of the
pleasantest times we ever passed"); saw Lloyd
again, but remained distrustful of him on account of the seeds of bitterness he had once
sown between the friends, and finally got home
very pleasantly : Mary a good deal fatigued,
finding the difference between going to a place
and coming from it, but not otherwise the
worse." "Lloyd has written me a fine letter of
friendship," says Lamb soon after his return,
"all about himself and Sophia, and love and

cant, which I have not answered. I have not given up the idea of writing to him, but it will be done very plainly and sincerely, without acrimony."

They found the Wordsworths (the poet and his sister, that is, for he was not yet married, though just about to be) lodging near their own quarters, saw much of them, pioneered them through Bartlemy Fair; and now on Mary's part was formed that intimacy with Dorothy which led to her being their constant visitor and sometimes their house-guest when she was in London.

As great a contrast in most respects to Dorothy Wordsworth, as the whole range of womankind could have furnished, was Mary's other friend and correspondent, Sara Stoddart, afterwards Mrs. Hazlitt. Sara was the only daughter of a retired lieutenant in the navy, a Scotchman who had settled down on a little property at Winterslow, near Salisbury, which she ultimately inherited. She was a young lady with a business-like determination to marry, and with many suitors; but, far from following the old injunction to be off with the old love before being on with the new, she always cautiously kept the old love dangling till she was quite sure the new was the more eligible. Mary's letters to her have happily been preserved and published by Miss Stoddart's grandson, Mr. W.

Carew Hazlitt, in his *Mary and Charles Lamb*.
The first, dated September 21, 1803, was written after Miss Stoddart had been staying with
the Lambs, and when a decision had been arrived at that she should accompany her only
brother, Dr. Stoddart, to Malta, where he had
just been appointed King's Advocate. Mary's
spelling, and here and there even a little slip in
the matter of grammar, have been retained as
seeming part of the individuality of the letters : —

"I returned from my visit yesterday and was
very much pleased to find your letter ; for I
have been very anxious to hear how you are
going on. I could hardly help expecting to see
you when I came in ; yet though I should have
rejoiced to have seen your merry face again, I
believe it was better as it was, upon the whole ;
and all things considered, it is certainly better
you should go to Malta. The terms you are
upon with your lover [a Mr. Turner, to whom
she was engaged] does (as you say it will) appear wondrous strange to me ; however, as I
cannot enter into your feelings I certainly can
have nothing to say to it, only that I sincerely
wish you happy in your own way, however odd
that way may appear to me to be. I would
begin now to advise you to drop all correspondence with William [not William Hazlitt,

but an earlier admirer]; but, as I said before, as I cannot enter into your feelings and views of things, *your ways not being my ways*, why should I tell you what I would do in your situation? So, child, take thy own ways and God prosper thee in them!

"One thing my advising spirit must say : use as little secresy as possible ; make a friend of your sister-in-law; you know I was not struck with her at first sight, but, upon your account, I have watched and marked her very attentively, and while she was eating a bit of cold mutton in our kitchen we had a serious conversation. From the frankness of her manner I am convinced she is a person I could make a friend of ; why should not you? We talked freely about you : she seems to have a just notion of your character and will be fond of you if you will let her."

After instancing the misunderstanding between her own mother and aunt already quoted, Mary continues :—

"My aunt and my mother were wholly unlike you and your sister, yet in some degree theirs is the secret history, I believe, of all sisters-in-law, and you will smile when I tell you I think myself the only woman in the world who could live with a brother's wife and make a real friend of her, partly from early observation of the unhappy example I have just given you, and partly from a knack I know I have of looking into people's real characters and never expecting them to act out of it — never expecting another to do as I would in the same case. When you leave your mother, and say if you never see her again you shall feel no remorse, and when you make a *jewish* bargain with your *lover*, all this gives me no offense, because it is your nature and your temper, and I do not expect or want you to be otherwise than you are. I love you for the good that is in you and look for no change.

" *But* certainly you ought to struggle with the evil that does most easily beset you — a total want of politeness in behavior — I would say modesty of behavior, but that I should not convey to you my idea of the word modesty; for I certainly do not mean that you want *real modesty*, and what is usually called false or mock modesty I certainly do not wish you to possess; yet I trust you know what I mean well enough. *Secresy*, though you appear all frankness, is certainly a grand failing of yours; it is likewise your *brother's*, and, therefore, a family failing. By secresy I mean you both want the habit of telling each other at the moment everything that happens, where you go and what you do — that free communication of letters and opinions just as they arrive, as Charles and I do, and which is, after all, the only ground-work of friendship. Your brother, I will answer for it, will never tell his wife or his sister all that is in his mind; he will receive letters and not [mention it]. This is a fault Mrs. Stoddart can never [tell him of], but she can and will feel it, though on the whole and in every other respect she is happy with him. Begin, for God's sake, at the first and tell her everything that passes. At first she may hear you with indifference, but in time this will gain her affection and confidence; show her all your letters (no matter if she does not show hers). It is a pleasant thing for a friend to put into one's hand a letter just fresh from the post. I would even say, begin with showing her this, but that is freely written and loosely, and some apology ought to be made for it which I know not how to make, for I must write freely or not at all.

"If you do this well she will tell your brother, you will say; and what then, quotha? It will beget a freer communication amongst you, which is a thing devoutly to be wished.

"God bless you and grant you may preserve your integrity and remain unmarried and penniless, and make William a good and happy wife."

No wonder Mary's friendships were so stable and so various, with this knack of hers of looking into another's real character and never expecting him or her to act out of it, or to do as she would in the same case; taking no offense, looking for no change and asking for no other explanation than that it was her friend's nature. It s an epitome of social wisdom and of generous sentiment.

Coleridge had long been in bad health and worse spirits; and what he had first ignorantly used as a remedy had now become his tyrant — opium; for a time the curse of his life and the blight of his splendid powers. Sometimes

> Adown Lethean streams his spirit drifted;

sometimes he was stranded "in a howling wilderness of ghastly dreams," waking and sleeping, followed by deadly languors which opium caused and cured and caused again, driving him round in an accursed circle. He came up to London at the beginning of 1804, was much with the Lambs if not actually their guest, and finally decided to try change and join his friend Dr. Stoddart in Malta, where he landed April 18th. Mary, full of earnest and affectionate solicitude, sent a letter by him to Sara Stoddart, who had already arrived, bespeaking a warm and indulgent welcome for her suffering friend: —

"I will just write a few hasty lines to say Coleridge is setting off sooner than we expected, and I every moment expect him to call in one of his great hurrys for this. We rejoiced with exceeding great joy to hear of your safe arrival. I hope your brother will return home in a few years a very rich man. Seventy pounds in one fortnight is a pretty beginning.

"I envy your brother the pleasure of seeing Coleridge drop in unexpectedly upon him; we talk — but it is but wild and idle talk — of following him. He is to get my brother some snug little place of a thousand a year, and we are to leave all and come and live among ye. What a pretty dream!

"Coleridge is very ill. I dread the thoughts of his long voyage. Write as soon as he arrives whether *he* does or not, and tell me how he is. . . .

"He has got letters of recommendation to Governor Ball and God knows who; and he will talk and talk and be universally admired. But I wish to write for him a *letter of recommendation* to Mrs. Stoddart and to yourself to take upon ye, on his first arrival, to be kind, affectionate nurses; and mind, now, that you perform this duty faithfully and write me a good account of yourself. Behave to him as you would to me or to Charles if we came sick and unhappy to you.

"I have no news to send you; Coleridge will tell you how we are going on. Charles has lost the newspaper [an engagement on the *Morning Post*, which Coleridge had procured for him], but what we dreaded as an evil has proved a great blessing, for we have both strangely recovered our health and spirits since this has happened; and I hope, when I write next, I shall be able to tell you Charles has begun something which will produce a little money, for it is not well to be *very poor*, which we certainly are at this present writing.

"I sit writing here and thinking almost you will see it to-morrow; and what a long, long time it will be ere you receive this! When I saw your letter I fancy'd you were even just then in the first bustle of a new reception, every moment seeing new faces and staring at new objects, when, at that time, everything had become familiar to you; and the strangers, your new dancing partners, had perhaps become gossiping fire-side friends. You tell me of your gay, splendid doings; tell me, likewise, what manner of home-life you lead. Is a quiet evening in a Maltese drawing-room as pleasant as those we have passed in Mitre Court and Bell Yard? Tell me all about it, everything pleasant and everything unpleasant that befalls you.

"I want you to say a great deal about yourself.

Are you happy? and do you not repent going out?
I wish I could see you for one hour only.

"Remember me affectionately to your sister
and brother, and tell me when you write if Mrs.
Stoddart likes Malta and how the climate agrees
with her and with thee.

"We heard you were taken prisoners, and
for several days believed the tale.

"How did the pearls and the fine court finery
bear the fatigues of the voyage, and how often
have they been worn and admired?

"Rickman wants to know if you are going to
be married yet. Satisfy him in that little particular when you write.

"The Fenwicks send their love and Mrs.
Reynolds her love, and the little old lady her
best respects.

"Mrs. Jeffries, who I see now and then, talks
of you with tears in her eyes, and when she
heard you was taken prisoner, Lord! how
frightened she was. She has heard, she tells
me, that Mr. Stoddart is to have a pension of
two thousand a year whenever he chooses to return to England.

"God bless you and send you all manner of
comforts and happinesses."

Mrs. Reynolds was another "little old lady,"
a familiar figure at the Lambs' table. She had
once been Charles' school-mistress; had made

an unfortunate marriage, and would have gone
under in the social stream but for his kindly
hand. Out of their slender means he allowed
her £30 a year. She tickled Hood's fancy
when he too became a frequent guest there;
and he has described her as formal, fair and
flaxen-wigged like an elderly wax doll, speaking
as if by an artificial apparatus, through some
defect in the palate, and with a slight limp and
a twist occasioned by running too precipitately
down Greenwich Hill in her youth! She remembered Goldsmith, who had once lent her
his *Deserted Village.*

In those days of universal warfare and priva-
teering it was an anxious matter to have a friend
tossing in the Bay of Biscay, gales and storms
apart; so that tidings from Sara had been eagerly watched for : —

"Your letter," writes Mary, "which contained
the news of Coleridge's arrival, was a most welcome one; for we had begun to entertain very
unpleasant apprehensions for his safety; and
your kind reception of the forlorn wanderer
gave me the greatest pleasure, and I thank you
for it in my own and my brother's name. I
shall depend upon you for hearing of his welfare, for he does not write himself; but as long
as we know he is safe and in such kind
friends' hands we do not mind. Your letters,

my dear Sara, are to me very, very precious
ones. They are the kindest, best, most natural
ones I ever received. The one containing the
news of the arrival of Coleridge is, perhaps, the
best I ever saw ; and your old friend Charles is
of my opinion. We sent it off to Mrs. Coleridge and the Wordsworths — as well because
we thought it our duty to give them the first
notice we had of our dear friend's safety, as that
we were proud of showing our Sara's pretty letter.

"The letters we received a few days after
from you and your brother were far less welcome ones. I rejoiced to hear your sister is
well, but I grieved for the loss of the dear baby,
and I am sorry to find your brother is not so successful as he expected to be ; and yet I am almost tempted to wish his ill fortune may send
him over to us again. He has a friend, I understand, who is now at the head of the Admiralty ; why may he not return and make a fortune
here ?

"I cannot condole with you very sincerely
upon your failure in the fortune-making way. If
you regret it, so do I. But I hope to see you a
comfortable English wife ; and the forsaken, forgotten William, of English-partridge memory, I
have still a hankering after. However, I thank
you for your frank communication and I beg

you will continue it in future; and if I do not agree with a good grace to your having a Maltese husband, I will wish you happy, provided you make it a part of your marriage articles that your husband shall allow you to come over sea and make me one visit; else may neglect and overlookedness be your portion while you stay there.

"I would condole with you when the misfortune has befallen your poor leg; but such is the blessed distance we are at from each other that I hope, before you receive this, you have forgot it ever happened.

"Our compliments to the high ton at the Maltese court. Your brother is so profuse of them to me that, being, as you know, so unused to them, they perplex me sadly; in future I beg they may be discontinued. They always remind me of the free and I believe very improper letter I wrote to you while you were at the Isle of Wight [that already given advising frankness]. The more kindly you and your brother and sister took the impertinent advice contained in it, the more certain I feel that it was unnecessary, and, therefore, highly improper. Do not let your brother compliment me into the memory of it again.

"My brother has had a letter from your mother which has distressed him sadly — about the postage of some letters being paid by my brother. Your silly brother, it seems, has informed your mother (I did not think your brother could have been so silly) that Charles had grumbled on paying the said postage. The fact was, just at that time we were very poor, having lost the *Morning Post*, and we were beginning to practice a strict economy. My brother, who never makes up his mind whether he will be a miser or a spendthrift, is at all times a strange mixture of both [rigid in those small economies which enabled him to be not only just but generous on small means]." "Of this failing the even economy of your correct brother's temper makes him an ill judge. The miserly part of Charles, at that time smarting under his recent loss, then happened to reign triumphant ; and he would not write or let me write so often as he wished because the postage cost two and fourpence. Then came two or three of your poor mother's letters nearly together; and the two and fourpences he wished but grudged to pay for his own he was forced to pay for hers. In this dismal distress he applied to Fenwick to get his friend Motley to send them free from Portsmouth. This Mr. Fenwick could have done for half a word's speaking ; but this he did not do ! Then Charles foolishly and unthinkingly complained to your brother in a half-serious, half-joking way; and your brother has wickedly and with malice aforethought told your mother. Oh, fye upon him! what will your mother think of us?

"I, too, feel my share of blame in this vexatious business, for I saw the unlucky paragraph in my brother's letter; and I had a kind of foreboding that it would come to your mother's ears, although I had a higher idea of your brother's good sense than I find he deserved. By entreaties and prayer I might have prevailed on my brother to say nothing about it. But I make a point of conscience never to interfere or cross my brother in the humor he happens to be in. It always appears to me to be a vexatious kind of tyranny that women have no business to exercise over men, which, merely because, *they having a better judgment*, they have power to do. Let *men* alone and at last we find they come round to the right way which *we*, by a kind of intuition, perceive at once. But, better, far better that we should let them often do wrong than that they should have the torment of a monitor always at their elbows.

"Charles is sadly fretted now, I know, at what to say to your mother. I have made this long preamble about it to induce you, if possible, to reinstate us in your mother's good graces.

Say to her it was a jest misunderstood; tell her
Charles Lamb is not the shabby fellow she and
her son took him for, but that he is, now and
then, a trifle whimsical or so. I do not ask
your brother to do this, for I am offended with
him for the mischief he has made.

"I feel that I have too lightly passed over
the interesting account you sent me of your
late disappointment. It was not because I did
not feel and completely enter into the affair
with you. You surprise and please me with
the frank and generous way in which you deal
with your lovers, taking a refusal from their so
prudential hearts with a better grace and more
good humor than other women accept a suitor's
service. Continue this open, artless conduct,
and I trust you will at last find some man who
has sense enough to know you are well worth
risking a peaceable life of poverty for. I shall
yet live to see you a poor but happy English
wife.

"Remember me most affectionately to Coleridge, and I thank you again and again for all
your kindness to him. To dear Mrs. Stoddart
and your brother I beg my best love; and to
you all I wish health and happiness and a *soon*
return to old England.

"I have sent to Mr. Burrel's for your kind
present, but unfortunately he is not in town. I

am impatient to see my fine silk handkerchiefs, and I thank you for them not as a present, for I do not love presents, but as a remembrance of your old friend.   Farewell.

"I am, my best Sara,

"Your most affectionate friend,

"Mary Lamb."

"Good wishes and all proper remembrances from old nurse, Mrs. Jeffries, Mrs. Reynolds, Mrs. Rickman, etc. Long live Queen Hoop-oop-oop-oo and all the old merry phantoms."

Sara Stoddart returned to England before the year was out. Coleridge remained in Malta, filling temporarily, at the request of Sir Alexander Ball, Governor of the island, the post of Public Secretary till the end of September, 1805, when his friends lost track of him altogether for nearly a year; during which he visited Paris, wandered through Italy, Sicily, Cairo, and saw Vesuvius in December, when "the air was so consolidated with a massy cloud-curtain that it appeared like a mountain in basso-relievo in an interminable wall of some pantheon;" and after narrowly escaping imprisonment at the hands of Napoleon, suddenly reappeared amongst his friends in the autumn of 1806.

To the Wordsworths, brother and sister and young wife — for the three were one in heart —

this year of 1805 had been one of overwhelming sorrow. Their brother John, the brave and able ship's captain, who yet loved "all quiet things" as dearly as William, "although he loved more silently," and was wont to carry that beloved brother's poems to sea and con them to the music of the winds and waves; whose cherished scheme, so near fulfilment, it was to realize enough to settle in a cottage at Grasmere and devote his earnings to the poet's use, so that he might pursue his way unharassed by a thought of money, — this brother was shipwrecked on the Bill of Portland just as he was starting, and whilst the ship was yet in the pilot's hands, on what was to have been, in how different a sense, his last voyage.

> Six weeks beneath the moving sea
> He lay in slumber quietly,
> Unforced by wind or wave
> To quit the ship for which he died
> (All claims of duty satisfied);
> And there they found him at her side,
> And bore him to the grave.

After waiting a while in silence before a grief of such magnitude, Mary wrote to Dorothy Wordsworth. She speaks as one acquainted with a life-long sorrow, yet who has learned to find its companionship not bitter: —

"I thank you, my kind friend, for your most

comfortable letter; till I saw your own handwriting I could not persuade myself that I
should do well to write to you, though I have
often attempted it; but I always left off dissatisfied with what I had written, and feeling that
I was doing an improper thing to intrude upon
your sorrow. I wished to tell you that you
would one day feel the kind of peaceful state of
mind and sweet memory of the dead which you
so happily describe as now almost begun; but
I felt that it was improper and most grating to
the feeling of the afflicted to say to them that
the memory of their affliction would in time become a constant part, not only of their dream,
but of their most wakeful sense of happiness.
That you would see every object with and
through your lost brother, and that that would
at last become a real and everlasting source of
comfort to you, I felt and well knew from my
own experience in sorrow; but till you yourself
began to feel this I didn't dare tell you so; but
I send you some poor lines which I wrote under
this conviction of mind and before I heard
Coleridge was returning home. I will tran-
scribe them now, before I finish my letter, lest
a false shame prevent me then, for I know they
are much worse than they ought to be, written
as they were with strong feeling and on such a
subject; every line seems to me to be bor-

rowed; but I had no better way of expressing
my thoughts, and I never have the power of
altering or amending anything I have once laid
aside with dissatisfaction : —

> Why is he wandering on the sea?
> Coleridge should now with Wordsworth be.
> By slow degrees he'd steal away
> Their woe and gently bring a ray
> (So happily he'd time relief)
> Of comfort from their very grief.
> He'd tell them that their brother dead,
> When years have passed o'er their head,
> Will be remembered with such holy,
> True and perfect melancholy,
> That ever this lost brother John
> Will be their heart's companion.
> His voice they'll always hear,
> His face they'll always see;
> There's naught in life so sweet
> As such a memory.

Thus for a moment are we permitted to see
that, next to love for her brother, the memory
of her dead mother and friendship for Coleridge
were the deep and sacred influences of Mary's
life.

CHAPTER VII.

1805–6. — Æt. 41–2.

The letter to Miss Wordsworth called forth a response ; but, alas ! Mary was in sad exile when it arrived, and Charles, with a heart full of grief, wrote for her : —

"14th June, 1805.

"Your long, kind letter has not been thrown away (for it has given me great pleasure to find you are all resuming your old occupations and are better) ; but poor Mary, to whom it is addressed, cannot yet relish it. She has been attacked by one of her severe illnesses and is at present *from home*. Last Monday week was the day she left me, and I hope I may calculate upon having her again in a month or little more. I am rather afraid late hours have, in this case, contributed to her indisposition. . . . I have

5

every reason to suppose that this illness, like all the former ones, will be but temporary; but I cannot always feel so. Meantime she is dead to me, and I miss a prop. All my strength is gone, and I am like a fool, bereft of her coöperation. I dare not think lest I should think wrong, so used am I to look up to her in the least as in the biggest perplexity. To say all that I know of her would be more than I think anybody could believe or even understand; and when I hope to have her well again with me it would be sinning against her feelings to go about to praise her, for I can conceal nothing that I do from her. She is older and wiser and better than I, and all my wretched imperfections I cover to myself by resolutely thinking on her goodness. She would share life and death, Heaven and hell, with me. She lives but for me; and I know I have been wasting and teasing her life for five years past incessantly with my cursed drinking and ways of going on. But even in this upbraiding of myself I am offending against her, for I know that she has clung to me for better for worse; and if the balance has been against her hitherto it was a noble trade. . . .

"I cannot resist transcribing three or four lines which poor Mary made upon a picture (a 'Holy Family') which we saw at an auction only

one week before she left home. She was then
beginning to show signs of ill boding. They
are sweet lines, and upon a sweet picture ; but
I send them only as the last memorial of her : —

VIRGIN AND CHILD, L. da Vinci.

> Maternal lady, with thy virgin grace,
> Heaven-born thy Jesus seemeth sure,
>   And thou a virgin pure.
> Lady most perfect, when thy angel face
> Men look upon, they wish to be
> A Catholic, Madonna fair, to worship thee.

" You had her lines about the ' Lady Blanch.'
You have not had some which she wrote upon
a copy of a girl from Titian, which I had hung
up where that print of Blanch and the Abbess
(as she beautifully interpreted two female figures from L. da Vinci) had hung in our room.
'Tis light and pretty : —

> Who art thou, fair one, who usurp'st the place
> Of Blanch, the lady of the matchless grace?
> Come, fair and pretty, tell to me
> Who in thy life-time thou might'st be?
> Thou pretty art and fair,
> But with the Lady Blanch thou never must compare.
> No need for Blanch her history to tell;
> Whoever saw her face, they there did read it well;
> But when I look on thee, I only know
> There lived a pretty maid some hundred years ago.

" This is a little unfair, to tell so much about
ourselves and to advert so little to your letter,

so full of comfortable tidings of you all. But my own cares press pretty close upon me and you can make allowances. That you may go on gathering strength and peace is my next wish to Mary's recovery.

"I had almost forgot your repeated invitation. Supposing that Mary will be well and able, there is another *ability* which you may guess at which I cannot promise myself. In prudence we ought not to come. This illness will make it still more prudential to wait. It is not a balance of this way of spending our money against another way, but an absolute question of whether we shall stop now or go on wasting away the little we have got beforehand, which my wise conduct has already encroached upon one-half."

Pity it is that the little poem on the "Lady Blanch" should have perished, as I fear it has, if it contained as "sweet lines" as the foregoing.

Little more than a month after this (July 27) Charles writes cheerfully to Manning:—

"My old housekeeper has shown signs of convalescence and will shortly resume the power of the keys, so I shan't be cheated of my tea and liquors. Wind in the west, which promotes tranquillity. Have leisure now to anticipate seeing thee again. Have been taking leave [it was a very short leave] of tobacco in a rhyming address. Had thought *that vein* had long since closed up. Find I can rhyme and reason too. Think of studying mathematics to restrain the fire of my genius, which George Dyer recommends. Have frequent bleedings at the nose, which shows plethoric. Maybe shall try the sea myself, that great scene of wonders. Got incredibly sober and regular; shave oftener and hum a tune to signify cheerfulness and gallantry.

" Suddenly disposed to sleep, having taken a quart of peas with bacon and stout. Will not refuse Nature, who has done such things for me !

" Nurse ! don't call me unless Mr. Manning comes. — What ! the gentleman in spectacles ? — Yes.

"*Dormit.* C. L.

" Saturday, hot noon."

But although Mary was sufficiently recovered to return home at the end of the summer, she continued much shaken by the severity of this attack, and so also did her brother all through the autumn; as the following letters to Sara Stoddart, and still more one already quoted (pp. 99–100), show : —

"September, 1805.

"Certainly you are the best letter-writer (besides writing the best hand) in the world. I have just been reading over again your two long letters and I perceive they make me very envious. I have taken a brand-new pen and put on my *spectacles*, and am peering with all my might to see the lines in the paper, which the sight of your even lines had well-nigh tempted me to rule; and I have moreover taken two pinches of snuff extraordinary to clear my head, which feels more cloudy than common this fine, cheerful morning.

"All I can gather from your clear and, I have no doubt, faithful history of Maltese politics is that the good doctor, though a firm friend, an excellent fancier of brooches, a good husband, an upright advocate, and, in short, all that they say upon tombstones (for I do not recollect that they celebrate any fraternal virtues there), — yet is he but a *moody* brother; that your sister-in-law is pretty much like what all sisters-in-law have been since the first happy invention of the marriage state; that friend Coleridge has undergone no alteration by crossing the Atlantic [geography was evidently no part of Captain Starkey's curriculum], for his friendliness to you as well as the oddities you mention are just what one ought to look for from him; and that

you, my dear Sara, have proved yourself just as
unfit to flourish in a little proud garrison town
as I did shrewdly suspect you were before you
went there.

"If I possibly can I will prevail upon Charles
to write to your brother by the conveyance you
mention ; but he is so unwell I almost fear the
fortnight will slip away before I can get him in
the right vein. Indeed, it has been sad and
heavy times with us lately. When I am pretty
well his low spirits throw me back again ; and
when he begins to get a little cheerful, then I
do the same kind office for him. I heartily
wish for the arrival of Coleridge ; a few such
evenings as we have sometimes passed with
him would wind us up and set us going again.

"Do not say anything when you write of our
low spirits ; it will vex Charles. You would
laugh or you would cry, perhaps both, to see us
sit together looking at each other with long and
rueful faces, and saying ' How do you do ?' and
' How do you do ?' then we fall a-crying and
say we will be better on the morrow. He says
we are like toothache, and his friend gum-boil,
which, though a kind of ease, is but an uneasy
kind of ease, a comfort of rather an uncomfortable sort.

"I rejoice to hear of your mother's amend-
ment ; when you can leave her with any satis-

faction to yourself — which, as her sister, I think I understand by your letter, is with her, I hope you may soon be able to do — let me know upon what plan you mean to come to town. Your brother proposed your being six months in town and six with your mother; but he did not then know of your poor mother's illness. By his desire I inquired for a respectable family for you to board with, and from Captain Burney I heard of one I thought would suit you at that time. He particularly desires I would not think of your being with us, not thinking, I conjecture, the house of a single man *respectable* enough. Your brother gave me most unlimited orders to domineer over you, to be the inspector of all your actions, and to direct and govern you with a stern voice and a high hand; to be, in short, a very elder brother over you. Does the hearing of this, my meek pupil, make you long to come to London? I am making all the proper inquiries, against the time, of the newest and most approved modes (being myself mainly ignorant in these points) of etiquette and nicely-correct, maidenly manners.

"But to speak seriously. I mean, when we meet, that we will lay our heads together and consult and contrive the best way of making the best girl in the world the fine lady her brother wishes to see her; and believe me, Sara,

it is not so difficult a matter as one is apt to
imagine. I have observed many a demure lady
who passes muster admirably well, who, I think,
we could easily learn to imitate in a week or
two. We will talk of these things when we
meet. In the meantime I give you free leave
to be happy and merry at Salisbury in any way
you can. Has the partridge season opened any
communication between you and William? As
I allow you to be imprudent till I see you, I
shall expect to hear you have invited him to
taste his own birds. Have you scratched him
out of your will yet? Rickman is married, and
that is all the news I have to send you. I seem,
upon looking over my letter again, to have written too lightly of your distresses at Malta; but
however I may have written, believe me I enter
very feelingly into all your troubles. I love you
and I love your brother; and between you, both
of whom, I think, have been to blame, I know
not what to say; only this I say, try to think as
little as possible of past miscarriages; it was
perhaps so ordered by Providence that you
might return home to be a comfort to your
mother."

No long holiday trip was to be ventured on
while Mary continued thus shaken and de-
pressed. "We have been to two tiny excursions this summer, for three or four days each,

to a place near Harrow and to Egham, where Cooper's Hill is, and that is the total history of our rustication this year," Charles tells Wordsworth. In October Mary gives a slightly better account of herself : —

"I have made many attempts at writing to you, but it has always brought your troubles and my own so strongly into my mind, that I have been obliged to leave off and make Charles write for me. I am resolved now, however few lines I write, this shall go ; for I know, my kind friend, you will like once more to see my own handwriting.

"I have been for these few days past in rather better spirits, so that I begin almost to feel myself once more a living creature and to hope for happier times ; and in that hope I include the prospect of once more seeing my dear Sara in peace and comfort in our old garret. How did I wish for your presence to cheer my drooping heart when I returned home from banishment!

"Is your being with or near your poor dear mother necessary to her comfort? Does she take any notice of you? And is there any prospect of her recovery? How I grieve for her, for you ! . . .

"I went to the Admiralty, about your mother's pension ; from thence I was directed to an office in Lincoln's Inn. . . . They informed me it could not be paid to any person but Mr. Wray without a letter of attorney. . . . Do not let us neglect this business, and make use of me in any way you can.

"I have much to thank you and your kind brother for. I kept the dark silk, as you may suppose. You have made me very fine; the brooch is very beautiful. Mrs. Jeffries wept for gratitude when she saw your present; she desires all manner of thanks and good wishes. Your maid's sister has gone to live a few miles from town. Charles, however, found her out and gave her the handkerchief.

"I want to know if you have seen William and if there is any prospect in future there. All you said in your letter from Portsmouth that related to him was so burnt in the fumigating that we could only make out that it was unfavorable, but not the particulars; tell us again how you go on or if you have seen him. I conceit affairs will somehow be made up between you at last.

"I want to know how your brother goes on. Is he likely to make a very good fortune, and in how long a time? And how is he in the way of home comforts — I mean is he very happy with Mrs. Stoddart? This was a question I could not ask while you were there, and perhaps is not a fair one now; but I want to know how you all went on, and, in short, twenty little foolish questions, that one ought, perhaps, rather to ask when we meet than to write about. But do make me a little acquainted with the inside of the good doctor's house and what passes therein.

"Was Coleridge often with you? or did your brother and Col. argue long arguments, till between the two great arguers there grew a little coolness? or perchance the mighty friendship between Coleridge and your sovereign Governor, Sir Alexander Ball, might create a kind of jealousy; for we fancy something of a coolness did exist, from the little mention of C. ever made in your brother's letters.

"Write us, my good girl, a long, gossiping letter answering all these foolish questions — and tell me any silly thing you can recollect; any, the least particular, will be interesting to us, and we will never tell tales out of school; but we used to wonder and wonder how you all went on; and when you was coming home we said, 'Now we shall hear all from Sara.'

"God bless you, my dear friend. . . If you have sent Charles any commissions he has not executed write me word — he says he has lost or mislaid a letter desiring him to inquire about a wig. Write two letters — one of busi-

ness and pensions and one all about Sara Stoddart and Malta.

"We have got a picture of Charles ; do you
think your brother would like to have it ? If
you do, can you put us in a way how to send
it ? "

Mary's interest in her friend and her friend's
affairs is so hearty one cannot choose but share
it, and would gladly see what "the best letter-
writer in the world" had to tell of Coleridge
and Stoddart and the long arguments and little
jealousies ; and whether "William" had continued to dangle on, spite of distance and dis-
couragement ; and even to learn that the old
lady received her pension and her wig in safety.
But curiosity must remain unsatisfied, for none
of Miss Stoddart's letters have been preserved.

"The picture of Charles" was, we may feel
pretty sure, one which William Hazlitt painted
this year of Lamb "in the costume of a Vene-
tian senator." It is, on all accounts, a peculiarly
interesting portrait. Lamb was just thirty ; and
it gives, on the whole, a striking impression of
the nobility and beauty of form and feature
which characterized his head, and partly realizes
Proctor's description — "a countenance so full
of sensibility that it came upon you like a new
thought which you could not help dwelling upon
afterwards ;" though the subtle lines which

gave that wondrous sweetness of expression to the mouth are not fully rendered. Compared with the drawing by Hancock, done when Lamb was twenty-three, engraved in Cottle's *Early Recollections of Coleridge*, each may be said to corroborate the truth of the other, allowing for difference of age and aspect, — Hancock's being in profile, Hazlitt's (of which there is a good lithograph in Barry Cornwall's *Memoir*) nearly full-face. The print from it prefixed to Fitzgerald's *Lamb* is almost unrecognizable. It was the last time Hazlitt took a brush in hand, his grandson tells us; and it comes as a pleasant surprise — an indication that he was too modest in estimating his own gifts as a painter; and that the freshness of feeling and insight he displayed as an art critic were backed by some capacity for good workmanship.

It was whilst this portrait was being painted that the acquaintance between Lamb and Hazlitt ripened into an intimacy which, with one or two brief interruptions, was to be fruitful, invigorating on both sides and life-long. Hazlitt was at this time staying with his brother John, a successful miniature painter and a member of the Godwin circle, much frequented by the Lambs.

"It is not well to be very poor, which we certainly are at this present," Mary had lately written. This it was which spurred her on to undertake her first literary venture, the *Tales from Shakespeare.* The nature of the malady from which she suffered made continuous mental exertion distressing and probably injurious ; so that without this spur she would never, we may be sure, have dug and planted her little plot in the field of literature, and made of it a sweet and pleasant place for the young, where they may play and be nourished, regardless of time and change. The first hint of any such scheme occurs in a letter to Sara Stoddart dated April 22, 1806, written the very day she had left the Lambs : —

"I have heard that Coleridge was lately going through Sicily to Rome with a party ; but that, being unwell, he returned back to Naples. We think there is some mistake in this account and that his intended journey to Rome was in his former jaunt to Naples. If you know that at that time he had any such intention will you write instantly? for I do not know whether I ought to write to Mrs. Coleridge or not.

"I am going to make a sort of promise to myself and to you that I will write you kind of journal-like letters of the daily what-we-do matters, as they occur. This day seems to me a kind of new era in our time. It is not a birthday, nor a new year's day, nor a leave-off-smoking day ; but it is about an hour after the time of leaving you, our poor Phœnix, in the Salisbury stage, and Charles has just left me to go to his lodgings [a room to work in free from the distraction of constant visitors, just hired experimentally], and I am holding a solitary consultation with myself as to how I shall employ myself.

"Writing plays, novels, poems and all manner of such-like vaporing and vaporish schemes are floating in my head, which, at the same time, aches with the thought of parting from you, and is perplext at the idea of I cannot tell what-about notion that I have not made you half so comfortable as I ought to have done, and a melancholy sense of the dull prospect you have before you on your return home. Then I think I will make my new gown ; and now I consider the white petticoat will be better candle-light work ; and then I look at the fire and think if the irons was but down I would iron my gowns — you having put me out of conceit of mangling.

So much for an account of my own confused head ; and now for yours. Returning home from the inn, we took that to pieces and canvassed you, as you know is our usual custom. We agreed we should miss you sadly, and that you had been what you yourself discovered, *not at all in our way;* and although, if the postmaster should happen to open this, it would appear to him to be no great compliment ; yet you, who enter so warmly into the interior of our affairs, will understand and value it as well as what we likewise asserted, that since you have been with us you have done but one foolish thing : *vide* Pinckhorn. (Excuse my bad Latin, if it should chance to mean exactly contrary to what I intend.) We praised you for the very friendly way in which you regarded all our whimsies, and, to use a phrase of Coleridge, *understood us.* We had, in short, no drawback on our eulogy on your merit except lamenting the want of respect you have to yourself, the want of a certain dignity of action (you know what I mean), which — though it only broke out in the acceptance of the old justice's book, and was, as it were, smothered and almost extinct while you were here — yet is it so native a feeling in your mind that you will do whatever the present moment prompts you to do, that I wish you would take that one slight offense seriously to heart, and make it a part of your daily consideration to drive this unlucky propensity, root and branch, out of your character. Then, mercy on us, what a perfect little gentlewoman you will be ! ! !

"You are not yet arrived at the first stage of your journey ; yet have I the sense of your absence so strong upon me that I was really thinking what news I had to send you, and what had happened since you had left us. Truly nothing, except that Martin Burney met us in Lincoln's Inn Fields and borrowed fourpence, of the repayment of which sum I will send you due notice.

"*Friday.* — Last night I told Charles of your matrimonial overtures from Mr. White and of the cause of that business being at a *standstill*. Your generous conduct in acquainting Mr. White with the vexatious affair at Malta highly pleased him. He entirely approves of it. You would be quite comforted to hear what he said on the subject.

"He wishes you success; and when Coleridge comes will consult with him about what is best to be done. But I charge you be most strictly cautious how you proceed yourself. Do not give Mr. W. any reason to think you indiscreet; let him return of his own accord and keep the probability of his doing so full in your mind; so, I mean, as to regulate your whole conduct by that expectation. Do not allow yourself to see or in any way renew your acquaintance with William, nor do any other silly thing of that kind; for you may depend upon it he will be a kind of spy upon you, and if he observes nothing that he disapproves of you will certainly hear of him again in time.

"Charles is gone to finish the farce [*Mr. H.*] and I am to hear it read this night. I am so uneasy between my hopes and fears of how I shall like it that I do not know what I am doing. I need not tell you so, for before I send this I shall be able to tell you all about it. If I think it will amuse you I will send you a copy. *The bed was very cold last night.*

"I have received your letter and am happy to hear that your mother has been so well in your absence, which I wish had been prolonged a little, for you have been wanted to copy out the farce, in the writing of which I made many an unlucky blunder.

"The said farce I carried (after many consultations of who was the most proper person to perform so important an office) to Wroughton, the manager of Drury Lane. He was very civil to me ; said it did not depend upon himself, but that he would put it into the proprietor's hands, and that we should certainly have an answer from them.

"I have been unable to finish this sheet before, for Charles has taken a week's holliday from his lodging to rest himself after his labor, and we have talked of nothing but the farce night and day; but yesterday I carried it to Wroughton, and since it has been out of the way our minds have been a little easier. I wish you had been with us to have given your opinion. I have half a mind to scribble another copy and send it you. I like it very much, and cannot help having great hopes of its success.

"I would say I was very sorry for the death of Mr. White's father, but not knowing the good old gentleman, I cannot help being as well satisfied that he is gone, for his son will feel rather lonely, and so, perhaps, he may chance to visit again Winterslow. You so well describe your brother's grave lecturing letter that you make me ashamed of part of mine. I would fain rewrite it, leaving out my '*sage advice;*' but if I begin another letter something may fall out to prevent me from finishing it, and, therefore, skip over it as well as you can; it shall be the last I ever send you.

"It is well enough when one is talking to a friend to hedge in an odd word by way of counsel now and then; but there is something mighty irksome in its staring upon one in a letter, where one ought only to see kind words and friendly remembrances.

"I have heard a vague report from the Dawes (the pleasant-looking young lady we called upon was Miss Dawe) that Coleridge returned back to Naples; they are to make further inquiries and let me know the particulars. We have seen little or nothing of Manning since you went.

Your friend George Burnet calls as usual for Charles *to point out something for him.* I miss you sadly, and but for the fidget I have been in about the farce, I should have missed you still more. I am sorry you cannot get your money; continue to tell us all your perplexities, and do not mind being called Widow Blackacre.

"Say all in your mind about your *lover;* now Charles knows of it, he will be as anxious to hear as me. All the time we can spare from talking of the characters and plot of the farce, we talk of you. I have got a fresh bottle of brandy to-day; if you were here you should have a glass, *three parts brandy,* so you should. I bought a pound of bacon to-day, not so good as yours. I wish the little caps were finished. I am glad the medicines and the cordials bore the fatigue of their journey so well. I promise you I will write often, and *not mind the postage.* God bless you. Charles does *not* send his love because he is not here. *Write as often as ever you can.* Do not work too hard."

There is a little anecdote of Sara Stoddart, told by her grandson, which helps to mitigate our astonishment at Mary's too hospitable suggestion in regard to the brandy. Lieutenant Stoddart would sometimes, while sipping his grog, say to his children : " John, will you have some ? " " No, thank you, father." " Sara,

will you?" "Yes, please, father." "Not,"
adds Mr. Hazlitt, "that she ever indulged to
excess, but she was that sort of woman." Very
far, certainly, from "the perfect little gentlewoman" Mary hoped one day to see her; but
friendly, not without brains, with a kindly heart,
and her worst qualities such, surely, as spread
themselves freely on the surface, but strike no
deep or poisonous roots. "Do not mind being
called Widow Blackacre," says Mary, alluding to
one of the characters in Wycherley's *Plain
Dealer.* It certainly was not gratifying to be
likened to that "perverse, bustling, masculine,
pettifogging and litigious" lady, albeit Macaulay
speaks of her as Wycherley's happiest creation.

When Hazlitt returned to Wem, Lamb sent
him his first letter full of friendly gossip : —

". . . We miss you, as we foretold we
should. One or two things have happened
which are beneath the dignity of epistolary
communication, but which, seated about our
fireside at night (the winter hands of pork have
begun), gesture and emphasis might have
talked into some importance. Something about
Rickman's wife, for instance ; how tall she is,
and that she visits pranked up like a Queen of
the May with green streamers ; a good-natured
woman though, which is as much as you can expect from a friend's wife, whom you got ac-

quainted with a bachelor. Something, too,
about Monkey [Louisa Martin], which can't so
well be written ; how it set up for a fine lady,
and thought it had got lovers and was obliged
to be convinced of its age from the parish register, where it was proved to be only twelve,
and an edict issued that it should not give itself
airs yet this four years ; and how it got leave to
be called Miss by grace. These and such like
hows were in my head to tell you, but who can
write? Also how Manning is come to town in
spectacles, and studies physic ; is melancholy,
and seems to have something in his head
which he don't impart. Then, how I am going
to leave off smoking. . . . You disappoint
me in passing over in absolute silence the Blenheim Leonardo. Didn't you see it? Excuse a
lover's curiosity. I have seen no pictures of
note since, except Mr. Dawe's gallery. It is
curious to see how differently two great men
treat the same subject, yet both excellent in
their way. For instance, Milton and Mr. Dawe.
Mr. D. has chosen to illustrate the story of
Samson exactly in the point of view in which
Milton has been most happy : the interview
between the Jewish hero, blind and captive,
and Delilah. Milton has imagined his locks
grown again, strong as horse-hair or porcu-
pine's bristles ; doubtless shaggy and black, as

being hairs ' of which a nation armed contained
the strength.'   I don't remember he *says* black;
but could Milton imagine them to be yellow?
Do you?   Mr. Dawe, with striking originality
of conception, has crowned him with a thin
yellow wig; in color precisely like Dyson's, in
curl and quantity resembling Mrs. Professor's
(Godwin's wife); his limbs rather stout, about
such a man as my brother or Rickman, but no
Atlas nor Hercules, nor yet so long as Dubois,
the clown of Sadler's Wells.   This was judicious, taking the spirit of the story rather than
the fact; for doubtless God could communicate
national salvation to the trust of flax and tow
as well as hemp and cordage, and could draw
down a temple with a golden tress as soon as
with all the cables of the British navy.

"Wasn't you sorry for Lord Nelson?   I have
followed him in fancy ever since I saw him in
Pall Mall (I was prejudiced against him before),
looking just as a hero should look, and I have
been very much cut about it indeed.   He was
the only pretense of a great man we had.   Nobody is left of any name at all.   His secretary
died by his side.   I imagined him, a Mr. Scott,
to be the man you met at Hume's, but I learn
from Mrs. Hume it is not the same. . . . What
other news is there, Mary?   What puns have I
made in the last fortnight?   You never remem-

ber them. You have no relish for the comic.
'Oh, tell Hazlitt not to forget to send the
American Farmer. I dare say it's not as good
as he fancies, but a book's a book.' " . . .

Mary was no exclusive lover of her brother's
old folios, his "ragged veterans" and "midnight
darlings," but a miscellaneous reader with a
decided leaning to modern tales and adventures
— to "a story, well, ill or indifferently told, so
there be life stirring in it," as Elia has told.

It may be worth noting here that the Mr.
Scott mentioned above, who was not the secretary killed by Nelson's side, was his chaplain,
and, though not killed, he received a wound in
the skull of so curious a nature as to cause occasionally a sudden suspension of memory. In
the midst of a sentence he would stop abruptly,
losing, apparently, all mental consciousness;
and after a lapse of time would resume at the
very word with which he had left off, wholly
unaware of any breach of continuity; as one
who knew him has often related to me.

CHAPTER VIII.

The *Tales from Shakespeare.* — Letters to Sara Stoddart.

1806. — Æt. 42.

ONCE begun, the *Tales from Shakespeare* were worked at with spirit and rapidity. By May 10th Charles writes to Manning : —

"[Mary] says you saw her writings about the other day, and she wishes you should know what they are. She is doing for Godwin's bookseller twenty of Shakespeare's plays, to be made into children's tales. Six are already done by her, to wit : *The Tempest, A Winter's Tale, Midsummer Night's Dream, Much Ado about Nothing, The Two Gentlemen of Verona,* and *Cymbeline.* The *Merchant of Venice* is in forwardness. I have done *Othello* and *Macbeth,* and mean to do all the tragedies. I think it will be popular among the little people, besides money. It is to bring in sixty guineas. Mary has done them capitally, I think you'd think."

"Godwin's bookseller" was really Godwin himself, who at his wife's urgent entreaty had just started a "magazine" of children's books in Hanway street, hoping thus to add to his precarious earnings as an author. His own name was in such ill odor with the orthodox that he used his foreman's — Thomas Hodgkins — over the shop-door and on the title-pages, whilst the juvenile books which he himself wrote were published under the name of Baldwin. When the business was removed to Skinner street it was carried on in his wife's name.

"My tales are to be published in separate story-books," Mary tells Sara Stoddart. "I mean in single stories, like the children's little shilling books. I cannot send you them in manuscript, because they are all in the Godwins' hands; but one will be published very soon, and then you shall have it *all in print.* I go on very well, and have no doubt but I shall always be able to hit upon some such kind of job to keep going on. I think I shall get fifty pounds a year at the lowest calculation ; but as I have not yet seen any *money* of my own earning (for we do not expect to be paid till Christmas), I do not feel the good fortune that has so unexpectedly befallen me half so much as I ought to do. But another year, no doubt, I shall perceive it. . . Charles has written *Macbeth*, *Othello*, *King Lear*, and has begun *Hamlet;* you would like to see us, as we often sit writing on one table (but not on one cushion sitting), like Hermia and Helena in the *Midsummer Night's Dream;* or rather, like an old literary Darby and Joan, I taking snuff and he groaning all the while and saying he can make nothing of it, which he always says till he has finished, and then he finds out he has made something of it.

"If I tell you that you Widow Blackacre-ize you must tell me I *tale*-ize, for my tales seem to be all the subject-matter I write about; and when you see them you will think them poor little baby-stories to make such a talk about."

And a month later she says:— "The reason I have not written so long is that I worked and worked in hopes to get through my task before the holidays began; but at last I was not able, for Charles was forced to get them now, or he could not have any at all; and having picked out the best stories first, these latter ones take more time, being more perplext and unmanage-able. I have finished one to-day, which teazed me more than all the rest put together. They sometimes plague me as bad as your *lovers* do you. How do you go on, and how many new ones have you had lately?"

"Mary is just stuck fast in *All's Well that Ends Well*," writes Charles. "She complains of having to set forth so many female characters in boys' clothes. She begins to think Shakespeare must have wanted imagination ! I, to encourage her (for she often faints in the prosecution of her great work), flatter her with telling how well such and such a play is done. But she is stuck fast, and I have been obliged to promise to assist her."

At last Mary, in a postscript to her letter to Sara, adds : "I am in good spirits just at this present time, for Charles has been reading over the tale I told you plagued me so much, and he thinks it one of the very best. You must not mind the many wretchedly dull letters I have sent you ; for, indeed, I cannot help it ; my mind is always so wretchedly *dry* after poring over my work all day. But it will soon be over. I am cooking a shoulder of lamb (Hazlitt dines with us) ; it will be ready at 2 o'clock if you can pop in and eat a bit with us."

Mary took a very modest estimate of her own achievement ; but time has tested it, and passed it on to generation after generation of children, and the last makes it as welcome as the first. Hardly a year passes but a new edition is absorbed ; and not by children only, but by the young generally, for no better introduction to the study of Shakespeare can be desired. Of the twenty plays included in the two small volumes which were issued in January, 1807, fourteen — *The Tempest, A Midsummer Night's Dream, A Winter's Tale, Much Ado about Nothing, As You Like It, The Two Gentlemen of Verona, The Merchant of Venice, Cymbeline, All's Well that Ends Well, The Taming of the Shrew, The Comedy of Errors, Measure for Measure, Twelfth Night,* and *Pericles, Prince of Tyre* — were by Mary; and the remaining six, the great tragedies, by Charles. Her share was the more difficult and the less grateful, not only on account of the more "perplext and unmanageable" plots of the comedies, but also of the sacrifices entailed in converting witty dialogue into brief narrative. But she "constantly evinces a rare shrewdness and tact in her incidental criticisms, which show her to have been, in her way, as keen an observer of human nature as her brother," says Mr. Ainger in his preface to the *Golden Treasury* edition of the tales. "She" had "not lived so much among the wits and humorists of her day without learning some truths which helped her to interpret the two chief characters of *Much Ado about Nothing;* for instance: The hint Beatrice gave Benedict that he was a coward, by saying she would eat all he had killed, he did not regard, knowing himself to be a brave man; but there is nothing that great wits so much dread as the imputation of buffoonery, because

the charge comes sometimes a little too near
the truth ; therefore Benedict perfectly hated
Beatrice when she called him the prince's
jester." Very profound, too, is the casual
remark upon the conduct of Claudio and his
friends when the character of Hero is suddenly
blasted — conduct which has often perplexed
older readers for its heartlessness and insane
credulity : "The prince and Claudio left the
church without staying to see if Hero would
recover, or at all regarding the distress into
which they had thrown Leonato, *so hard-hearted
had their anger made them.*"

If one must hunt for a flaw to show critical
discernment, it is a pity that in *Pericles*, otherwise so successfully handled, with judicious
ignoring of what is manifestly not Shakespeare's, a beautiful passage is marred by the
omission of a word that is the very heart of the
simile : —

See how she 'gins to blow into life's flower again,

says Cerimon, as the seemingly dead Thaisa
revives. " See, she begins to blow into life
again," Mary has it.

The tales appeared first in eight sixpenny
numbers, but were soon collected in two small
volumes "embellished," or, as it turned out,
disfigured by twenty copper-plate illustrations,

of which, as of other attendant vexations, Lamb
complains in a letter to Wordsworth, dated January 29, 1807 : —

"We have booked off from the 'Swan and
Two Necks,' Lad Lane, this day (per coach),
the *Tales from Shakespeare.* You will forgive
the plates, when I tell you they were left to the
direction of Godwin, who left the choice of subjects to the bad baby [Mrs. Godwin], who from
mischief (I suppose) has chosen one from d——d
beastly vulgarity (vide *Merch. Venice*), when no
atom of authority was in the tale to justify it;
to another, has given a name which exists not
in the tale, Nic Bottom, and which she thought
would be funny, though in this I suspect *his*
hand, for I guess her reading does not reach
far enough to know Bottom's Christian name;
and one of Hamlet and grave-digging, a scene
which is not hinted at in the story, and you
might as well have put King Canute the Great,
reproving his courtiers. The rest are giants
and giantesses. Suffice it to save our taste and
damn our folly, that we left all to a friend, W.
G., who in the first place cheated me by putting
a name to them which I did not mean, but do
not repent, and then wrote a puff about their
simplicity, etc., to go with the advertisement as
in my name! Enough of this egregious dupery.
I will try to abstract the load of teasing circum-

stances from the stories, and tell you that I am answerable for *Lear, Macbeth, Timon, Romeo, Hamlet, Othello,* for occasionally a tail-piece or correction of grammar, for none of the cuts and all of the spelling. The rest is my sister's. We think *Pericles* of hers the best, and *Othello* of mine; but I hope all have some good. *As You Like It,* we like least. So much, only begging you to tear out the cuts and give them to Johnny as 'Mrs. Godwin's fancy' ! !

"I had almost forgot my part of the preface begins in the middle of a sentence, in last but one page, after a colon, thus —

: — which if they be happily so done, etc.

The former part hath a mere feminine turn, and does hold me up something as an instructor to young ladies, but upon my modesty's honor I wrote it not.

"Godwin told my sister that the 'baby' chose the subjects : a fact in taste."

Mary's preface sets forth her aim and her difficulties with characteristic good sense and simplicity. I have marked with a bracket the point at which, quite tired and out of breath, as it were, at the end of her labors, she put the pen into her brother's hand, that he might finish with a few decisive touches what remained to be said of their joint undertaking : —

6

PREFACE.

The following tales are meant to be submitted to the young reader as an introduction to the study of Shakespeare, for which purpose his words are used whenever it seemed possible to bring them in ; and in whatever has been added to give them the regular form of a connected story, diligent care has been taken to select such words as might least interrupt the effect of the beautiful English tongue in which he wrote ; therefore, words introduced into our language since his time have been as far as possible avoided.

In those tales which have been taken from the tragedies, as my young readers will perceive when they come to see the source from which these stories are derived, Shakespeare's own words, with little alteration, recur very frequently in the narrative as well as in the dialogue ; but in those made from the comedies I found myself scarcely ever able to turn his words into the narrative form ; therefore I fear in them I have made use of dialogue too frequently for young people not used to the dramatic form of writing. But this fault — if it be, as I fear, a fault — has been caused by my earnest wish to give as much of Shakespeare's own words as possible ; and if the "*He said*" and "*She said*," the question and the reply, should sometimes seem tedious to their young ears, they must pardon it, because it was the only way I knew of in which I could give them a few hints and little foretastes of the great pleasure which awaits them in their elder years, when they come to the rich treasures from which these small and valueless coins are extracted, pretending to no other merit than as faint and imperfect stamps of Shakespeare's matchless image. Faint and imperfect images they must be called, because the beauty of his language is too frequently destroyed by the necessity of changing many of his excellent words into words far less expressive of his true sense, to make it read something like prose; and even in some few places where his blank verse is given unaltered, as hoping from its simple plainness to cheat the young readers into the belief that they are reading prose, yet still, his language being transplanted from its own natural soil and wild, poetic garden, it must want much of its native beauty.

I have wished to make these tales easy reading for very young children. To the utmost of my ability I have constantly kept this in my mind; but the subjects of most of them made this a very difficult task. It was no easy matter to give the histories of men and women in terms familiar to the apprehension of a very

young mind. For young ladies, too, it has been
my intention chiefly to write, because boys are
generally permitted the use of their fathers'
libraries at a much earlier age than girls are,
they frequently having the best scenes of
Shakespeare by heart before their sisters are
permitted to look into this manly book; and
therefore, instead of recommending these tales
to the perusal of young gentlemen who can
read them so much better in the originals, I
must rather beg their kind assistance in explaining to their sisters such parts as are hardest for them to understand; and when they
have helped them to get over the difficulties,
then perhaps they will read to them.— carefully
selecting what is proper for a young sister's
ear — some passage which has pleased them in
one of these stories, in the very words of the
scene from which it is taken. And I trust they
will find that the beautiful extracts, the select
passages, they may choose to give their sisters
in this way will be much better relished and
understood from their having some notion of
the general story from one of these imperfect
abridgments, which, if they be fortunately so
done as to prove delightful to any of you, my
young readers, I hope will have no worse effect
upon you than to make you wish yourself a little
older, that you may be allowed to read the plays

at full length : such a wish will be neither peevish nor irrational. When time and leave of judicious friends shall put them into your hands, you will discover in such of them as are here abridged — not to mention almost as many more which are left untouched — many surprising events and turns of fortune, which for their infinite variety could not be contained in this little book, besides a world of sprightly and cheerful characters, both men and women, the humor of which I was fearful of losing if I attempted to reduce the length of them.

What these tales have been to you in childhood, that and much more it is my wish that the true plays of Shakespeare may prove to you in older years — enrichers of the fancy, strengtheners of virtue, a withdrawing from all selfish and mercenary thoughts, a lesson of all sweet and honorable thoughts and actions, to teach you courtesy, benignity, generosity, humanity ; for of examples teaching these virtues his pages are full.

If the "bad baby" chose the subjects, a stripling who was afterwards to make his mark in art executed them : a young Irishman, son of a leather-breeches maker, Mulready by name, whom Godwin and also Harris, Newberry's successor, were at this time endeavoring to help in his twofold struggle to earn a livelihood and

obtain some training in art (which he did chiefly
in the studio of Banks, the sculptor).   Some of
his early illustrations to the rhymed satirical
fables just then in vogue, such as *The Butter-
fly's Ball* and the *Peacock at Home*, show humor
as well as decisive artistic promise.   But the
young designer seems to have collapsed altogether under the weight of Shakespeare's crea-
tions ; and whoever looks at the goggle-eyed
ogre of the pantomime species called Othello,
as well as at the plates Lamb specifies, will not
wonder at his disgust.   Curiously enough they
have been attributed to Blake — those in the
edition of 1822, that is, which are identical with
those of 1807 and 1816, — and as such figure in
booksellers' catalogues, with a correspondingly
high price attached to the volumes, notwithstanding the testimony to the contrary of Mr.
Sheepshanks, given in Stephens' *Masterpieces of
Mulready*.   Engraved by Blake they may have
been, and hence may have here and there
traces of Blakelike feeling and character ; for
though he was fifty at the time these were executed, he still and always had to win his bread
more often by rendering with his graver the
immature or brainless conceptions of others,
than by realizing those of his own teeming and
powerful imagination.

The success of the tales was decisive and
immediate.   New editions were called for in

1810, 1816 and 1822; but in concession, no doubt, to Lamb's earnest remonstrances, only a certain portion of each contained the obnoxious plates; the rest were issued with "merely a beautiful head of our immortal dramatist, from a much-admired painting by Zoust," as Godwin's advertisement put it. Subsequently an edition, with designs by Harvey, remained long in favor and was reprinted many times. In 1837, Robert, brother of the more famous George Cruikshank, illustrated the book, and there was prefixed a memoir of Lamb by J. W. Dalby, a friend of Leigh Hunt and contributor to the *London Journal*. The *Golden Treasury* edition, already spoken of, has a dainty little frontispiece by Du Maurier, with which Lamb would certainly have found no fault.

No sooner were the *Tales* out of hand than Mary began a fresh task, as Charles tells Manning in a letter written at the end of the year (1806), wherein also is a glimpse of our friend Mr. Dawe, not to be here omitted: "Mr. Dawe is turned author; he has been in such a way lately — Dawe the painter, I mean — he sits and stands about at Holcroft's and says nothing; then sighs and leans his head on his hand. I took him to be in love; but it seems he was only meditating a work, *The Life of Morland*. The young man is not used to composition."

CHAPTER IX.

Correspondence with Sara Stoddart.—Hazlitt.—A Courtship and Wedding, at which Mary is Bridesmaid.

1806–8. — Æt. 42–4.

To return to domestic affairs, as faithfully
reported to Sara by Mary whilst the *Tales* were
in progress:—

"MAY 14, 1806.

"No intention of forfeiting my promise, but
want of time has prevented me from continuing
my *journal.* You seem pleased with the long,
stupid one I sent, and, therefore, I shall continue to write at every opportunity. The reason why I have not had any time to spare is
because Charles has given himself some hollidays after the hard labor of finishing his farce ;
and, therefore, I have had none of the evening
leisure I promised myself. Next week he
promises to go to work again. I wish he may
happen to hit upon some new plan to his mind
for another farce [*Mr. H.* was accepted, but not

yet brought out]. When once begun, I do not
fear his perseverance, but the hollidays he has
allowed himself I fear will unsettle him. I look
forward to next week with the same kind of
anxiety I did to the new lodging. We have
had, as you know, so many teazing anxieties of
late, that I have got a kind of habit of foreboding that we shall never be comfortable, and that
he will never settle to work, which I know is
wrong, and which I will try with all my might
to overcome; for certainly if I could but see
things as they really are, our prospects are considerably improved since the memorable day of
Mrs. Fenwick's last visit. I have heard nothing of that good lady or of the Fells since you
left us.

"We have been visiting a little to Norris',
Godwin's, and last night we did not come home
from Captain Burney's till two o'clock; the
Saturday night was changed to Friday, because
Rickman could not be there to-night. We had
the best *tea things*, and the litter all cleared
away, and everything as handsome as possible,
Mrs. Rickman being of the party. Mrs. Rickman is much increased in size since we saw
her last, and the alteration in her strait shape
wonderfully improves her. Phillips was there,
and Charles had a long batch of cribbage with
him, and upon the whole we had the most

chearful evening I have known there for a long
time. To-morrow we dine at Holcroft's. These
things rather fatigue me; but I look for a quiet
week next week and hope for better times. We
have had Mrs. Brooks and all the Martins, and
we have likewise been there, so that I seem to
have been in a continual bustle lately. I do not
think Charles cares so much for the Martins as
he did, which is a fact you will be glad to hear,
though you must not name them when you
write; always remember, when I tell you anything about them, not to mention their names
in return.

"We have had a letter from your brother by
the same mail as yours, I suppose; he says he
does not mean to return till summer, and that
is all he says about himself; his letter being
entirely filled with a long story about Lord
Nelson — but nothing more than what the
papers have been full of — such as his last
words, etc. Why does he tease you with so
much *good advice?* Is it merely to fill up his
letters, as he filled ours with Lord Nelson's
exploits? or has any new thing come out against
you? Has he discovered Mr. Curse-a-rat's correspondence? I hope you will not write to that
news-sending gentleman any more. I promised
never more to give my *advice*, but one may be
allowed to *hope* a little; and I also hope you

will have something to tell me soon about Mr. White. Have you seen him yet? I am sorry to hear your mother is not better, but I am in a hoping humor just now, and I cannot help hoping that we shall all see happier days. The bells are just now ringing for the taking of the *Cape of Good Hope*.

"I have written to Mrs. Coleridge to tell her that her husband is at Naples. Your brother slightly named his being there, but he did not say that he had heard from him himself. Charles is very busy at the office; he will be kept there to-day till seven or eight o'clock; and he came home very *smoky and drinky* last night, so that I am afraid a hard day's work will not agree very well with him.

"O dear! what shall I say next? Why, this I will say next, that I wish you was with me; I have been eating a mutton chop all alone, and I have just been looking in the pint porter-pot, which I find quite empty, and yet I am still very dry. If you was with me we would have a glass of brandy and water; but it is quite impossible to drink brandy and water by one's self; therefore, I must wait with patience till the kettle boils. I hate to drink tea alone; it is worse than dining alone. We have got a fresh cargo of biscuits from Captain Burney's. I have ——

"MAY 14. — Here I was interrupted, and a long, tedious interval has intervened, during which I have had neither time nor inclination to write a word. The lodging, that pride of your heart and mine, is given up, and *here he is again* — Charles, I mean — as unsettled and undetermined as ever. When he went to the poor lodging after the holidays I told you he had taken, he could not endure the solitariness of them, and I had no rest for the sole of my foot till I promised to believe his solemn protestations that he could and would write as well at home as there. Do you believe this?

"I have no power over Charles; he will do what he will do. But I ought to have some little influence over myself; and, therefore, I am most manfully resolving to turn over a new leaf with my own mind. Your visit, though not a very comfortable one to yourself, has been of great use to me. I set you up in my fancy as a kind of *thing* that takes an interest in my concerns; and I hear you talking to me, and arguing the matter very learnedly, when I give way to despondency. You shall hear a good account of me and the progress I make in altering my fretful temper to a calm and quiet one. It is but once being thoroughly convinced one is wrong, to make one resolve to do so no more; and I know my dismal faces have been almost as great a drawback upon Charles' comfort, as his feverish, teazing ways have been upon mine. Our love for each other has been the torment of our lives hitherto. I am most seriously intending to bend the whole force of my mind to counteract this, and I think I see some prospect of success.

"Of Charles ever bringing any work to pass at home, I am very doubtful; and of the farce succeeding, I have little or no hope; but if I could once get into the way of being cheerful myself, I should see an easy remedy in leaving town and living cheaply, almost wholly alone; but till I do find we really are comfortable alone, and by ourselves, it seems a dangerous experiment. We shall certainly stay where we are till after next Christmas; and in the meantime, as I told you before, all my whole thoughts shall be to *change* myself into just such a chearful soul as you would be in a lone house, with no companion but your brother, if you had nothing to vex you, nor no means of wandering after *Curse-a-rats*. Do write soon; though I write all about myself, I am thinking all the while of you, and I am uneasy at the length of time it seems since I heard from you. Your mother and Mr. White is running continually in my head; and this *second winter* makes me think how cold, damp and forlorn your solitary house will feel to you.   I would your feet were perched up again on our fender."   . . .

If ever a woman knew how to keep on the right side of that line which, in the close companionship of daily life, is so hard to find, the line that separates an honest, faithful friend from "a torment of a monitor," and could divine when and how to lend a man a helping hand against his own foibles, and when to forbear and wait patiently, that woman was Mary Lamb.

Times were changed indeed since Lamb could speak of himself as "alone, obscure, without a friend."   Now friends and acquaintances thronged round him, till rest and quiet were almost banished from his fire-side; and though they were banished for the most part by social pleasures he dearly loved — hearty, simple, intellectual pleasures — the best of talk, with no ceremony and the least of expense, yet they had to be paid for by Mary and himself in fevered nerves, in sleep curtailed and endless interruptions to work.   There were, besides, "social harpies who preyed on him for his liquors," whom he lacked firmness to shake off, in spite of those "dismal faces" consequent in Mary, of which she penitently accuses herself.

Apart from external distractions, the effort to write, especially any sort of task-work, was

often so painful to his irritable nerves that, as
he said, it almost "teazed him into a fever,"
whilst Mary's anxious love and close sympathy
made his distress her own. There is a letter
to Godwin deprecating any appearance of un-
friendliness in having failed to review his *Life
of Chaucer*, containing a passage on this subject,
which the lover of Lamb's writings and character (and who is one must needs be the other)
will ponder with peculiar interest:—

"You, by long habits of composition and a
greater command over your own powers, cannot
conceive of the desultory and uncertain way in
which I (an author by fits) sometimes cannot
put the thoughts of a common letter into sane
prose. Any work which I take upon myself as
an engagement will act upon me to torment;
e. g. when I have undertaken, as three or four
times I have, a school-boy copy of verses for
merchant tailors' boys at a guinea a copy, I
have fretted over them in perfect inability to
do them, and have made my sister wretched
with my wretchedness for a week together.
As to reviewing, in particular, my head is so
whimsical a head that I cannot, after reading
another man's book, let it have been never so
pleasing, give any account of it in any methodical way. I cannot follow his train. Something
like this you must have perceived of me in con-

versation. Ten thousand times I have confessed to you, talking of my talents, my utter
inability to remember, in any comprehensive
way, what I read. I can vehemently applaud
or perversely stickle at *parts*, but I cannot grasp
a whole. This infirmity may be seen in my
two little compositions, the tale and my play, in
both which no reader, however partial, can find
any story. . . . If I bring you a crude,
wretched paper on Sunday, you must burn it
and forgive me; if it proves anything better
than I predict, may it be a peace-offering of
sweet incense between us."

The two friends whose society was always
soothing were far away now. Coleridge, who
could always "wind them up and set them going
again," as Mary said, was still wandering they
knew not where on the Continent, and Manning
had at last carried out a long-cherished scheme
and gone to China for four years, which, however, stretched to twelve, as Lamb prophesied
it would.

"I didn't know what your going was till I
shook a last fist with you," says Lamb, "and
then 'twas just like having shaken hands with a
wretch on the fatal scaffold, for when you are
down the ladder you never can stretch out to
him again. Mary says you are dead, and
there's nothing to do but to leave it to time to

do for us in the end what it always does for those who mourn for people in such a case; but she'll see by your letter you are not quite dead. A little kicking and agony, and then — Martin Burney *took me out* a-walking that evening, and we talked of Manning, and then I came home and smoked for you; and at twelve o'clock came home Mary and Monkey Louisa from the play, and there was more talk and more smoking, and they all seemed first-rate characters because they knew a certain person. But what's the use of talking about 'em? By the time you'll have made your escape from the Kalmucks, you'll have stayed so long I shall never be able to bring to your mind who Mary was, who will have died about a year before, nor who the Holcrofts were. Me, perhaps, you will mistake for Phillips, or confound me with Mr. Dawe, because you saw us together. Mary, whom you seem to remember yet, is not quite easy that she had not a formal parting from you. I wish it had so happened. But you must bring her a token, a shawl or something, and remember a sprightly little mandarin for our mantel-piece as a companion to the child I am going to purchase at the museum. . . . O Manning, I am serious to sinking, almost, when I think that all those evenings which you have made so pleasant are gone, perhaps forever. . . . I will nurse the remembrance of your steadiness and quiet which used to infuse something like itself into our nervous minds. Mary used to call you our ventilator."

Mary's next letters to Miss Stoddart continue to fulfil her promise of writing a kind of journal : —

"JUNE 2ND.

"You say truly that I have sent you too many make-believe letters. I do not mean to serve you so again if I can help it. I have been very ill for some days past with the toothache. Yesterday I had it drawn, and I feel myself greatly relieved, but far from being easy, for my head and my jaws still ache ; and being unable to do any business, I would wish to write you a long letter to atone for my former offenses; but I feel so languid that I fear wishing is all I can do.

"I am sorry you are so worried with business, and I am still more sorry for your sprained ancle. You ought not to walk upon it. What is the matter between you and your good-natured maid you used to boast of ? and what the devil is the matter with your aunt ? You say she is discontented. You must bear with them as well as you can, for doubtless it is your poor mother's teazing that puts you all out of sorts. I pity you from my heart.

"We cannot come to see you this summer, nor do I think it advisable to come and incommode you when you for the same expense could come to us. Whenever you feel yourself disposed to run away from your troubles, come to us again. I wish it was not such a long, expensive journey, and then you could run backwards and forwards every month or two. I am very sorry you still hear nothing from Mr. White. I am afraid that is all at an end. What do you intend to do about Mr. Turner ? . . . . William Hazlitt, the brother of him you know, is in town. I believe you have heard us say we like him. He came in good time, for the loss of Manning made Charles very dull, and he likes Hazlitt better than anybody, except Manning. My toothache has moped Charles to death ; you know how he hates to see people ill. . . .

"When I write again you will hear tidings of the farce, for Charles is to go in a few days to the managers to inquire about it. But that must now be a next year's business too, even if it does succeed, so it's all looking forward and no prospect of present gain. But that's better than no hopes at all, either for present or future times. . . . Charles smokes still, and will smoke to the end of the chapter. Martin [Burney] has just been here. My *Tales* (*again*) and Charles' farce have made the boy mad to turn author, and he has made the *Winter's Tale* into a story ; but what Charles says of himself is really true of Martin, for he can *make nothing at all of it*, and I have been talking very eloquently this morning to convince him that nobody can write farces, etc., under thirty years of age ; and so I suppose he will go home and new-model his farce.

"What is Mr. Turner, and what is likely to come of him? And how do you like him? And what do you intend to do about it? I almost wish you to remain single till your mother dies, and then come and live with us, and we would either get you a husband or teach you how to live comfortably without. I think I should like to have you always, to the end of our lives, living with us ; and I do not know any reason why that should not be, except for the great fancy you seem to have for marrying, which after all is but a hazardous kind of affair ; but, however, do as you like ; every man knows best what pleases himself best.

"I have known many single men I should have liked in my life (*if it had suited them*) for a husband ; but very few husbands have I ever wished was mine, which is rather against the state in general ; but one never is disposed to envy wives their good husbands. So much for marrying — but, however, get married if you can.

"I say we shall not come and see you, and I feel sure we shall not; but if some sudden freak was to come into our wayward heads, could you at all manage? Your mother we should not mind, but I think still it would be so vastly inconvenient. I am certain we shall not come, and yet *you* may tell me when you write if it would be horribly inconvenient if we did; and do not tell me any lies, but say truly whether you would rather we did or not.

"God bless you, my dearest Sara! I wish for your sake I could have written a very amusing letter; but do not scold, for my head aches sadly. Don't mind my headache, for before you get this it will be well, being only from the pains of my jaws and teeth. Farewell."

"JULY 2ND.

"Charles and Hazlitt are going to Sadler's Wells, and I am amusing myself in their absence with reading a manuscript of Hazlitt's, but have laid it down to write a few lines to tell you how we are going on. Charles has begged a month's hollidays, of which this is the first day, and they are all to be spent at home. We thank you for your kind invitations, and were half inclined to come down to you; but after

mature deliberation and many wise consultations—such as you know we often hold—we
came to the resolution of staying quietly at
home, and during the hollidays we are both of
us to set stoutly to work and finish the tales.
We thought if we went anywhere and left them
undone they would lay upon our minds, and that
when we returned we should feel unsettled, and
our money all spent besides; and next summer
we are to be very rich, and then we can afford
a long journey somewhere; I will not say to
Salisbury, because I really think it is better for
you to come to us. But of that we will talk
another time.

"The best news I have to send you is that
the farce is accepted; that is to say, the manager has written to say it shall be brought out
when an opportunity serves. I hope that it
may come out by next Christmas. You must
come and see it the first night; for if it succeeds it will be a great pleasure to you, and if it
should not we shall want your consolation; so
you must come.

"I shall soon have done my work, and know
not what to begin next. Now, will you set
your brains to work and invent a story, either
for a short child's story, or a long one that
would make a kind of novel, or a story that
would make a play? Charles wants me to write

a play, but I am not over-anxious to set about it. But, seriously, will you draw me out a sketch of a story, either from memory of anything you have read, or from your own invention, and I will fit it up in some way or other? . . .

"I met Mrs. Fenwick at Mrs. Holcroft's the other day. She looked placid and smiling, but I was so disconcerted that I hardly knew how to sit upon my chair. She invited us to come and see her, but we did not invite her in return, and nothing at all was said in an explanatory sort, so that matter rests for the present." [Perhaps the little imbroglio was the result of some effort on Mary's part to diminish the frequency of the undesirable Mr. Fenwick's visits. He was a good-for-nothing; but his wife's name deserves to be remembered because she nursed Mary Wollstonecraft tenderly and devotedly in her last illness.] "I am sorry you are altogether so uncomfortable; I shall be glad to hear you are settled at Salisbury; that must be better than living in a lone house, companionless, as you are. I wish you could afford to bring your mother up to London, but that is quite impossible. Mrs. Wordsworth is brought to bed, and I ought to write to Miss Wordsworth and thank her for the information, but I suppose I shall defer it till another child is coming. I do so hate writing letters. I wish all my friends would come and live in town. It is not my dislike to writing letters that prevents my writing to you, but sheer want of time, I assure you; because you care not how stupidly I write so as you do but hear at the time what we are about.

"Let me hear from you soon, and do let me hear some good news, and don't let me hear of your walking with sprained ancles again; no business is an excuse for making yourself lame.

"I hope your poor mother is better, and auntie and maid jog on pretty well; remember me to them all in due form and order. Charles' love and our best wishes that all your little busy affairs may come to a prosperous conclusion."

                              "FRIDAY EVENING.

"They (Hazlitt and Charles) came home from Sadler's Wells so dismal and dreary dull on Friday evening that I gave them both a good scolding, *quite a setting to rights;* and I think it has done some good, for Charles has been very chearful ever since. I begin to hope the *home hollidays* will go on very well. Write directly, for I am uneasy about your *Lovers;* I wish something was settled. God bless you." . . .

Sara's lovers continued a source of lively if "uneasy" interest to Mary. The enterprising young lady had now another string to her bow; indeed, matters this time went so far that the question of settlements was raised, and Mary wrote a letter, in which her "advising spirit" shows itself as wise as it was unobtrusive, as candid as it was tolerant. Dr. Stoddart clearly estimated her judgment and tact, after his fashion, as highly as Coleridge and Wordsworth did after theirs. Mary wrote:—

"OCTOBER 22.

"I thank you a thousand times for the beautiful work you have sent me. I received the parcel from a strange gentleman yesterday. I like the patterns very much. You have quite set me up in finery; but you should have sent the silk handkerchief too; will you make a parcel of that and send it by the Salisbury coach? I should like to have it for a few days, because we have not yet been to Mr. Babb's, and that handkerchief would suit this time of year nicely. I have received a long letter from your brother on the subject of your intended marriage. I have no doubt but you also have one on this business; therefore it is needless to repeat what he says. I am well pleased to find that, upon the whole, he does not seem to see

it in an unfavorable light. He says that if Mr.
Dowling is a worthy man, he shall have no
objection to become the brother of a farmer;
and he makes an odd request to me, that I shall
set out to Salisbury to look at and examine into
the merits of the said Mr. D., and speaks very
confidently, as if you would abide by my determination. A pretty sort of an office, truly!
Shall I come? The objections he starts are
only such as you and I have already talked
over—such as the difference in age, education,
habits of life, etc.

"You have gone too far in this affair for any
interference to be at all desirable; and if you
had not, I really do not know what my wishes
would be. When you bring Mr. Dowling at
Christmas I suppose it will be quite time
enough for me to sit in judgment upon him;
but my examination will not be a very severe
one. If you fancy a very young man and he
likes an elderly gentlewoman; if he likes a
learned and accomplished lady and you like a
not very learned youth who may need a little
polishing, which probably he will never ac-
quire,—it is all very well, and God bless you
both together, and may you be both very long
in the same mind!

"I am to assist you too, your brother says, in
drawing up the marriage settlements; another

thankful office! I am not, it seems, to suffer you to keep too much money in your own power, and yet I am to take care of you in case of bankruptcy; and I am to recommend to you, for the better management of this point, the serious perusal of *Jeremy Taylor*, his opinion on the marriage state, especially his advice against *separate interests* in that happy state; and I am also to tell you how desirable it is that the husband should have the entire direction of all money concerns, except, as your good brother adds, in the case of his own family, when the money, he observes, is very properly deposited in Mrs. Stoddart's hands, she being better suited to enjoy such a trust than any other woman; and therefore it is fit that the general rule should not be extended to her.

"We will talk over these things when you come to town; and as to settlements, which are matters of which I — I never having had a penny in my own disposal — never in my life thought of; and if I had been blessed with a good fortune, and that marvelous blessing to boot, a good husband, I verily believe I should have crammed it all uncounted into his pocket. But thou hast a cooler head of thine own, and I dare say will do exactly what is expedient and proper; but your brother's opinion seems somewhat like Mr. Barwis', and I dare say you will take it into due consideration; yet, perhaps, an offer of your own money to take a farm may make *uncle* do less for his nephew, and in that case Mr. D. might be a loser by your generosity. Weigh all these things well, and if you can so contrive it, let your brother *settle* the *settlements* himself when he returns, which will most probably be long before you want them.

"You are settled, it seems, in the very house which your brother most dislikes. If you find this house very inconvenient, get out of it as fast as you can, for your brother says he sent you the fifty pounds to make you comfortable; and by the general tone of his letter I am sure he wishes to make you easy in money matters; therefore, why straiten yourself to pay the debt you owe him, which I am well assured he never means to take? Thank you for the letter, and for the picture of pretty little chubby nephew John. I have been busy making waiskoats and plotting new work to succeed the *Tales;* as yet I have not hit upon anything to my mind.

"Charles took an emendated copy of his farce to Mr. Wroughton, the manager, yesterday. Mr. Wroughton was very friendly to him and expressed high approbation of the farce; but there are two, he tells him, to come out before it; yet he gave him hopes that it will come out this season; but I am afraid you will not see it by Christmas. It will do for another jaunt for you in the spring. We are pretty well and in fresh spirits about this farce. Charles has been very good lately in the matter of *Smoking*.

"When you come bring the gown you wish to sell; Mrs. Coleridge will be in town then, and if she happens not to fancy it, perhaps some other person may.

"Coleridge, I believe, is gone home; he left us with that design, but we have not heard from him this fortnight. . . .

"My respects to Corydon, mother and aunty. Farewell. My best wishes are with you.

"When I saw what a prodigious quantity of work you had put into the finery, I was quite ashamed of my unreasonable request. I will never serve you so again, but I do dearly love worked muslin."

So Coleridge was come back at last. "He is going to turn lecturer, on Taste, at the Royal Institution," Charles tells Manning. And the farce came out and failed. "We are pretty stout about it," he says to Wordsworth; "but, after all, we had rather it had succeeded. You will see the prologue in most of the morning papers. It was received with such shouts as I never witnessed to a prologue. It was attempted to be encored. How hard!—a thing I merely did as a task, because it was wanted, and set no great store by; and *Mr. H.!!* The number of friends we had in the house, my brother and I being in public offices, was astonishing, but they yielded at length to a few hisses. A hundred hisses! (D——n the word! I write it like kisses—how different!) a hundred hisses outweigh a thousand claps. The former come more directly from the heart. Well, 'tis withdrawn, and there is an end. Better luck to us."

Sara's visit came to pass and proved an eventful one to her. For at the Lambs' she now saw frequently their new friend, quite another William than he of "English-partridge memory," William Hazlitt; and the intercourse between them soon drifted into a queer kind of courtship, and finally the courtship into marriage. Mary's next letters give piquant glimpses of the wayward course of their love-making. If her sympathies had been ready and unfailing in the case of the unknown lovers, Messrs. White, Dowling, Turner, and mysterious *Curse-a-rat*, this was an affair of deep and heartfelt interest :—

"OCT., 1807.

"I am two letters in your debt, but it has not been so much from idleness, as a wish to see how your comical love affair would turn out.

You know I made a pretense not to interfere, but like all old maids I feel a mighty solicitude about the event of love stories. I learn from the lover that he has not been so remiss in his duty as you supposed. His effusion and your complaints of his inconstancy crossed each other on the road. He tells me his was a very strange letter, and that probably it has affronted you. That it was a strange letter I can readily believe ; but that you were affronted by a strange letter is not so easy for me to conceive, that not being your way of taking things. But, however it may be, let some answer come either to him or else to me, showing cause why you do not answer him. And pray, by all means, preserve the said letter, that I may one day have the pleasure of seeing how Mr. Hazlitt treats of love.

" I was at your brother's on Thursday. Mrs. Stoddart tells me she has not written, because she does not like to put you to the expense of postage. They are very well. Little Missy thrives amazingly. Mrs. Stoddart conjectures she is in the family way again, and those kind of conjectures generally prove too true. Your other sister-in-law, Mrs. Hazlitt, was brought to bed last week of a boy, so that you are likely to have plenty of nephews and nieces. Yesterday evening we were at Rickman's, and who should we find there but Hazlitt ; though if you do not know it was his first invitation there, it will not surprise you as much as it did us. We were very much pleased, because we dearly love our friends to be respected by our friends. The most remarkable events of the evening were that we had a very fine pine-apple, that Mr. Phillips, Mr. Lamb and Mr. Hazlitt played at cribbage in the most polite and gentlemanly manner possible, and that I won two rubbers at whist.

"I am glad aunty left you some business to do. Our compliments to her and to your mother. Is it as cold at Winterslow as it is here ? How do the Lions go on ? I am better and Charles is tolerably well. Godwin's new tragedy [Antonio] will probably be damned the latter end of next week [which it was]. Charles has written the prologue. Prologues and epilogues will be his death. If you know the extent of Mrs. Reynolds' poverty, you will be glad to hear Mr. Norris has got ten pounds a year for her from the Temple Society. She will be able to make out pretty well now.

"Farewell. Determine as wisely as you can in regard to Hazlitt, and if your determination is to have him, Heaven send you many happy years together. If I am not mistaken I have concluded letters on the Corydon courtship with

this same wish. I hope it is not ominous of
change; for if I were sure you would not be
quite starved to death nor beaten to a mummy,
I should like to see Hazlitt and you come
together, if (as Charles observes) it were only
for the joke's sake. Write instantly to me."

"DEC. 21.

"I have deferred answering your last letter
in hopes of being able to give you some intelligence that might be useful to you; for I every
day expected that Hazlitt or you would communicate the affair to your brother; but as the
doctor is silent upon the subject, I conclude he
knows nothing of the matter. You desire my
advice, and therefore I tell you I think you
ought to tell your brother as soon as possible;
for at present he is on very friendly visiting
terms with Hazlitt, and, if he is not offended
by too long concealment, will do everything in
his power to serve you. If you chuse that I
should tell him I will, but I think it would come
better from you. If you can persuade Hazlitt
to mention it, that would be still better; for I
know your brother would be unwilling to give
credit to you, because you deceived yourself in
regard to Corydon. Hazlitt, I know, is shy of
speaking first; but I think it of such great
importance to you to have your brother friendly

7

in the business that, if you can overcome his reluctance, it would be a great point gained. For you must begin the world with ready money —at least an hundred pounds; for if you once go into furnished lodgings, you will never be able to lay by money to buy furniture. If you obtain your brother's approbation he might assist you, either by lending or otherwise. I have a great opinion of his generosity where he thinks it would be useful.

"Hazlitt's brother is mightily pleased with the match, but he says you must have furniture, and be clear in the world at first setting out, or you will be always behind-hand. He also said he would give you what furniture he could spare. I am afraid you can bring but few things away from your own house. What a pity that you have laid out so much money on your cottage! that money would just have done. I most heartily congratulate you on having so well got over your first difficulties; and now that it is quite settled, let us have no more fears. I now mean not only to hope and wish, but to persuade myself that you will be very happy together. Endeavor to keep your mind as easy as you can. You ought to begin the world with a good stock of health and spirits; it is quite as necessary as ready money at first setting out. Do not teize yourself about coming to town. When your brother learns how things are going on, we shall consult him about meetings and so forth; but at present, any hasty step of that kind would not answer, I know. If Hazlitt were to go down to Salisbury, or you were to come up here without consulting your brother, you know it would never do. Charles is just come into dinner : he desires his love and best wishes."

Perhaps the reader will, like Mary, be curious to see one of the lover's letters in this "comical love affair." Fortunately one, the very one, it seems, which Sara's crossed, and was preserved at Mary's particular request, is given in the Hazlitt *Memoirs*, and runs thus:—

"MY DEAR LOVE:

"Above a week has passed and I have received no letter—not one of those letters 'in which I live or have no life at all.' What is become of you? Are you married, hearing that I was dead (for so it has been reported)? or are you gone into a nunnery? or are you fallen in love with some of the amorous heroes of Boccaccio? Which of them is it? Is it Chynon, who was transformed from a clown into a lover, and learned to spell by the force of beauty? or with Lorenzo, the lover of Isabella, whom her three brethren hated (as your brother does me), who was a merchant's clerk? or with Federigo Alberigi, an honest gentleman who ran through his fortune, and won his mistress by cooking a fair falcon for her dinner, though it was the only means he had left of getting a dinner for himself? This last is the man; and I am the more persuaded of it because I think I won your good liking myself by giving you an entertainment—of sausages, when I had no money to buy them with. Nay, now, never deny it! Did not I ask your consent that very night after, and did you not give it? Well, I should be confoundedly jealous of those fine gallants if I did not know that a living dog is better than a dead lion; though, now I think of it, Boccaccio does not in general make much of his lovers; it is his women who are so delicious. I almost wish I had lived in those times and had been a little *more amiable*. Now, if a woman had written the book it would not have had this effect upon me: the men would have been heroes and angels, and the women nothing at all. Isn't there some truth in that? Talking of departed loves, I met my old flame the other day in the street. I did dream of her *one* night since, and only one; every other night I have had the same dream I have had for these two months past. Now, if you are at all reasonable this will satisfy you.

"*Thursday morning.*—The book is come. When I saw it I thought that you had sent it back in a huff, tired out by my sauciness and *coldness* and delays, and were going to keep an account of dimities and sayes, or to salt pork and chronicle small beer, as the dutiful wife of some fresh-looking rural swain; so that you cannot think how surprised and pleased I was to find them all done. I liked your note as well or better than the extracts; it is just such a note as such a nice rogue as you ought to write after the *provocation* you had received. I would not give a pin for a girl 'whose cheeks never tingle,' nor for myself if I could not make them tingle sometimes. Now, though I am always writing to you about 'lips and noses' and such sort of stuff, yet as I sit by my fire-side (which I generally do eight or ten hours a day) I oftener think of you in a serious, sober light. For, indeed, I never love you so well as when I think of sitting down with you to dinner on a boiled scrag of mutton and hot potatoes. You please my fancy more then than when I think of you in ——; no, you would never forgive me if I were to finish the sentence. Now I think of it, what do you mean to be dressed in when we are married? But it does not much matter! I wish you would let your hair grow; though perhaps nothing will be better than 'the same

air and look with which at first my heart was
took.' But now to business. I mean soon to
call upon your brother *in form*, namely, as soon
as I get quite well, which I hope to do in about
another *fortnight;* and then I hope you will
come up by the coach as fast as the horses can
carry you, for I long mightily to be in your
ladyship's presence to vindicate my character.
I think you had better sell the small house, I
mean that at £4 10s., and I will borrow £100,
so that we shall set off merrily, in spite of all
the prudence of Edinburgh.

"Good bye, little dear!"

Poor Sara! That "want of a certain dignity
of action," nay, of a due "respect for herself,"
which Mary lamented in her, had been discovered but too quickly by her lover and reflected
back, as it was sure to be, in his attitude toward
her.

Charles, also, as an interested and amused
spectator of the unique love affair, reports
progress to Manning in a letter of Feb. 26th,
·1808 : —

"Mary is very thankful for your remembrance
of her; and with the least suspicion of merce-
nariness, as the silk, the *symbolum materiale* of
your friendship, has not yet appeared. I think

Horace says somewhere, *nox longa*. I would not impute negligence or unhandsome delays to a person whom you have honored with your confidence ; but I have not heard of the silk or of Mr. Knox save by your letter. May be he expects the first advances ! or it may be that he has not succeeded in getting the article on shore, for it is among the *res prohibitæ et non nisi smuggle-ationis viâ fruendæ*. But so it is ; in the friendships between *wicked men* the very expressions of their good will cannot but be sinful. A treaty of marriage is on foot between William Hazlitt and Miss Stoddart. Something about settlements only retards it. She has somewhere about £80 a year, to be £120 when her mother dies. He has no settlement except what he can claim from the parish. *Paupeo est tamen, sed amat*. The thing is therefore in abeyance. But there is love a-both sides."

In the same month Mary wrote Sara a letter showing she was alive to the fact that a courtship which appeared to on-lookers, if not to the lover himself, much in the light of a good joke, was not altogether a reassuring commencement of so serious an affair as marriage. She had her misgivings, and no wonder, as to how far the easy-going, comfort-loving, matter-of-fact Sara was fit for the difficult happiness of life-long companionship with a man of ardent genius and morbid, splenetic temperament, to whom ideas were meat, drink and clothing, while the tangible entities bearing those names were likely to be precariously supplied. Still Mary liked both the lovers so well she could not choose but that hope should preponderate over fear. Meeting as they did by the Lambs' fire-side, each saw the other to the best advantage. For, in the glow of Mary's sympathy and faith, and the fine, stimulating atmosphere of Charles' genius, Hazlitt's shyness had first melted away; his thoughts had broken the spell of self-distrust that kept them pent in uneasy silence, and had learned to flow forth in a strong and brilliant current, whilst the lowering frown which so often clouded his handsome, eager face was wont to clear off. There, too, Sara's unaffected good sense and hearty, friendly nature had free play, and perhaps Mary's friendship even reflected on her a tinge of the ideal to veil the coarser side of her character:—

"I have sent your letter and drawing," [of Middleton Cottage, Winterslow, where Sara was living,] Mary writes, "off to Wem, [Hazlitt's father's in Shropshire,] where I conjecture Hazlitt is. He left town on Saturday afternoon without telling us where he was going. He seemed very impatient at not hearing from you. He was very ill, and I suppose is gone home to

his father's to be nursed. I find Hazlitt has
mentioned to you the intention which we had
of asking you up to town, which we were bent
on doing ; but, having named it since to your
brother, the doctor expressed a strong desire
that you should not come to town to be at any
other house but his own, for he said it would
have a very strange appearance. His wife's
father is coming to be with them till near the
end of April, after which time he shall have
full room for you. And if you are to be married he wishes that you should be married with
all the proper decorums *from his house*. Now,
though we should be most willing to run any
hazards of disobliging him if there were no
other means of your and Hazlitt's meeting, yet
as he seems so friendly to the match it would
not be worth while to alienate him from you
and ourselves too, for the slight accommodation which the difference of a few weeks would
make ; provided always, and be it understood,
that if you and H. make up your minds to be
married before the time in which you can be at
your brother's, our house stands open and most
ready at a moment's notice to receive you.
Only we would not quarrel unnecessarily with
your brother. Let there be a clear necessity
shown and we will quarrel with anybody's
brother.

"Now, though I have written to the above effect, I hope you will not conceive but that both my brother and I had looked forward to your coming with unmixed pleasure, and are really disappointed at your brother's declaration; for next to the pleasure of being married is the pleasure of making or helping marriages forward.

"We wish to hear from you that you do not take our seeming change of purpose in ill part, for it is but seeming on our part, for it was my brother's suggestion, by him first mentioned to Hazlitt and cordially approved by me; but your brother has set his face against it, and it is better to take him along with us in our plans, if he will good-naturedly go along with us, than not.

"The reason I have not written lately has been that I thought it better to leave you all to the workings of your own minds in this momentous affair, in which the inclinations of a by-stander have a right to form a wish, but not to give a vote.

"Being, with the help of wide lines, at the end of my last page, I conclude with our kind wishes and prayers for the best."

The wedding-day was fixed and Mary was to be bridesmaid.

"Do not be angry that I have not written to

you," she says. "I have promised your brother to be at your wedding, and that favor you must accept as an atonement for my offenses. You have been in no want of correspondence lately, and I wished to leave you both to your own inventions.

"The border you are working for me I prize at a very high rate, because I consider it as the last work you can do for me, the time so fast approaching that you must no longer work for your friends. Yet my old fault of giving away presents has not left me, and I am desirous of even giving away this your last gift. I had intended to have given it away without your knowledge, but I have intrusted my secret to Hazlitt and I suppose it will not remain a secret long, so I condescend to consult you.

"It is to Miss Hazlitt to whose superior claim I wish to give up my right to this precious worked border. Her brother William is her great favorite and she would be pleased to possess his bride's last work. Are you not to give the fellow-border to one sister-in-law, and therefore has she not a just claim to it? I never heard in the annals of weddings (since the days of Nausicaa, and she only washed her old gowns for that purpose) that the brides ever furnished the apparel of their maids. Besides, I can be completely clad in your work

without it ; for the spotted muslin will serve
both for cap and hat (*nota bene*, my hat is the
same as yours), and the gown you sprigged for
me has never been made up, therefore I can
wear that — or, if you like better, I will make
up a new silk which Manning has sent me from
China. Manning would like to hear I wore it
for the first time at your wedding. It is a very
pretty light color, but there is an objection
(besides not being your work, and that is a very
serious objection), and that is Mrs. Hazlitt tells
me that all Winterslow would be in an uproar
if the bridesmaid was to be dressed in anything
but white, and although it is a very light color,
I confess we cannot call it white, being a sort
of dead-whiteish bloom color. Then silk, perhaps, in a morning is not so proper, though the
occasion, so joyful, might justify a full dress.
Determine for me in this perplexity between
the sprig and the China-Manning silk. But do
not contradict my whim about Miss Hazlitt
having the border, for I have set my heart
upon the matter. If you agree with me in this,
I shall think you have forgiven me for giving
away your pin — that was a *mad* trick ; but I
had many obligations and no money. I repent
me of the deed, wishing I had it now to send to
Miss H. with the border ; and I cannot, will not
give her the doctor's pin ; for having never had

any presents from gentlemen in my young days,
I highly prize all they now give me, thinking
my latter days are better than my former.

"You must send this same border in your
own name to Miss Hazlitt, which will save me
the disgrace of giving away your gift, and make
it amount merely to a civil refusal.

"I shall have no present to give you on your
marriage, nor do I expect I shall be rich enough
to give anything to baby at the first christening ; but at the second or third child's I hope
to have a coral or so to spare out of my own
earnings. Do not ask me to be godmother, for
I have an objection to that ; but there is, I
believe, no serious duties attaching to a bridesmaid, therefore I come with a willing mind,
bringing nothing with me but many wishes,
and not a few hopes, and a very little fear of
happy years to come."

If, as may be hoped, the final decision was in
favor of the "dead-whiteish bloom, China-Manning" silk, the Winterslow folk were spared all
painful emotions on the subject, as the wedding
took place at St. Andrew's, Holborn (May-day
morning, 1808), Dr. and Mrs. Stoddart and
Charles and Mary Lamb the chief, perhaps the
only guests. The comedy of the courtship
merging into the solemnity of marriage was
the very occasion to put Lamb into one of his

wildest moods. "I had like to have been turned out several times during the ceremony," he confessed to Southey afterwards. "Anything awful makes me laugh. I misbehaved once at a funeral. Yet can I read about these ceremonies with pious and proper feelings. The realities of life only seem the mockeries."

CHAPTER X.

Mrs. Leicester's School. — A Removal. — *Poetry for Children.*

1807–9. — Æt. 43–45.

THE *Tales from Shakespeare* were no sooner finished than Mary began, as her letters show, to cast about for some new scheme which should realize an equally felicitous and profitable result. This time she drew upon her own invention; and in about a year a little volume of tales for children was written, called *Mrs. Leicester's School*, to which Charles also contributed. The stories, ten in number, seven by Mary and three by her brother, are strung on a connecting thread by means of an introductory "Dedication to the Young Ladies at Amwell School," who are supposed to beguile the dreariness of the first evening at a new school by each telling the story of her own life, at the suggestion of a friendly governess, who constitutes herself their "historiographer."

There is little or no invention in these tales; but a "tenderness of feeling and a delicacy of taste" — the praise is Coleridge's — which lift

them quite above the ordinary level of children's stories. And in no way are these qualities shown more than in the treatment of the
lights and shades, the failings and the virtues,
of the little folk, which appear in due and natural proportion ; but the faults are treated in a
kindly, indulgent spirit, not spitefully enhanced
as foils to shining virtue, after the manner of
some even of the best writers for children.
There are no unlovely impersonations of naugh-
tiness pure and simple, nor any equally unlove-
able patterns of priggish perfection. But the
sweetest touches are in the portrayal of the
attitude of a very young mind towards death,
affecting from its very incapacity for grief, or
indeed from any kind of realization, as in this
story of *Elizabeth Villiers*, for instance :—

"The first thing I can remember was my
father teaching me the alphabet from the letters
on a tombstone that stood at the head of my
mother's grave. I used to tap at my father's
study door : I think I now hear him say, 'Who
is there ? What do you want, little girl ? Go
and see mamma. Go and learn pretty letters.'
Many times in the day would my father lay
aside his books and his papers to lead me to
this spot, and make me point to the letters, and
then set me to spell syllables and words ; in
this manner, the epitaph on my mother's tomb

being my primer and my spelling-book, I learned to read.

"I was one day sitting on a step placed across the churchyard stile, when a gentleman passing by heard me distinctly repeat the letters which formed my mother's name, and then say 'Elizabeth Villiers' with a firm tone, as if I had performed some great matter. This gentleman was my Uncle James, my mother's brother; he was a lieutenant in the navy, and had left England a few weeks after the marriage of my father and mother, and now, returned home from a long sea-voyage, he was coming to visit my mother, no tidings of her decease having reached him, though she had been dead more than a twelvemonth.

"When my uncle saw me sitting on the stile, and heard me pronounce my mother's name, he looked earnestly in my face and began to fancy a resemblance to his sister, and to think I might be her child. I was too intent on my employment to notice him, and went spelling on. 'Who has taught you to spell so prettily, my little maid?' said my uncle. 'Mamma,' I replied; for I had an idea that the words on the tombstone were somehow a part of mamma, and that she had taught me. 'And who is mamma?' asked my uncle. 'Elizabeth Villiers,' I replied; and then my uncle called me his dear little niece, and said he would go with me to mamma; he took hold of my hand, intending to lead me home, delighted that he had found out who I was, because he imagined it would be such a pleasant surprise to his sister to see her little daughter bringing home her long-lost sailor uncle.

"I agreed to take him to mamma, but we had a dispute about the way thither. My uncle was for going along the road which led directly up to our house; I pointed to the churchyard and said that was the way to mamma. Though impatient of any delay, he was not willing to contest the point with his new relation; therefore he lifted me over the stile, and was then going to take me along the path to a gate he knew was at the end of our garden; but no, I would not go that way neither. Letting go his hand, I said, 'You do not know the way; I will show you;' and making what haste I could among the long grass and thistles, and jumping over the low graves, he said, as he followed what he called my *wayward steps:* —

"'What a positive little soul this niece of mine is! I knew the way to your mother's house before you were born, child.' At last I stopped at my mother's grave, and pointing to the tombstone said, 'Here is mamma!' in a voice of exultation, as if I had now convinced him I knew the way best. I looked up in his face to see him acknowledge his mistake; but oh! what a face of sorrow did I see! I was so frightened that I have but an imperfect recollection of what followed. I remember I pulled his coat, and cried 'Sir! sir!' and tried to move him. I knew not what to do. My mind was in a strange confusion; I thought I had done something wrong in bringing the gentleman to mamma to make him cry so sadly, but what it was I could not tell. This grave had always been a scene of delight to me. In the house my father would often be weary of my prattle and send me from him; but here he was all my own. I might say anything and be as frolicsome as I pleased here; all was cheerfulness and good humor in our visits to mamma, as we called it. My father would tell me how quietly mamma slept there, and that he and his little Betsy would one day sleep beside mamma in that grave; and when I went to bed, as I laid my little head on the pillow I used to wish I was sleeping in the grave with my papa and mamma, and in my childish dreams I used to fancy myself there; and it was a place within the ground, all smooth and soft and green. I never made out any figure of mamma, but still it was the tombstone and papa and the smooth, green grass, and my head resting on the elbow of my father." . . .

In the story called *The Father's Wedding Day*
the same strain of feeling is developed in a
somewhat different way, but with a like truth.
Landor praised it with such genial yet whimsical extravagance as almost defeats itself, in a
letter to Crabb Robinson, written in 1831 : "It
is now several days since I read the book you
recommended to me, *Mrs. Leicester's School*,
and I feel as if I owed you a debt in deferring
to thank you for many hours of exquisite
delight. Never have I read anything in prose
so many times over within so short a space of
time as *The Father's Wedding Day*. Most
people, I understand, prefer the first tale — in
truth a very admirable one — but others could
have written it. Show me the man or woman,
modern or ancient, who could have written this
one sentence: 'When I was dressed in my new
frock I wished poor mamma was alive, to see
how fine I was on papa's wedding day; and I
ran to my favorite station at her bed-room
door.' How natural in a little girl is this
incongruity — this impossibility! Richardson
would have given his Clarissa and Rousseau his
Heloïse to have imagined it. A fresh source
of the pathetic bursts out before us, and not a
bitter one. If your Germans can show us anything comparable to what I have transcribed, I
would almost undergo a year's gurgle of their

language for it. The story is admirable throughout, incomparable, inimitable."

The second tale — *Louisa Manners, or the
Farm-house* — has already been spoken of (page
11) ; for in Louisa's pretty prattle we have a
reminiscence of Mary's happiest childish days
among "the Brutons and the Gladmans" in
Hertfordshire; and in *Margaret Green, or the
Young Mahometan* (pages 13–14), of her more
sombre experiences with Grandmother Field at
Blakesware.

The tales contributed by Charles Lamb are
Maria Howe, or the Effect of Witch Stories,
which contains a weird and wonderful portrait
of Aunt Hetty; *Susan Yates, or First Going to
Church* (see pages 3–4) ; and *Arabella Hardy, or
the Sea Voyage*.

It may be worth noting that Mary signs her
little prelude, the *Dedication to the Young
Ladies*, with the initials of her boy-favorite,
Martin Burney; a pretty indication of affection
for him.

Many years after the appearance of *Mrs.
Leicester's School* Coleridge said to Allsop:
"It at once soothes and amuses me to think —
nay, to know — that the time will come when
this little volume of my dear and well-nigh
oldest friend, Mary Lamb, will be not only
enjoyed but acknowledged as a rich jewel in

the treasury of our permanent English literature; and I cannot help running over in my mind the long list of celebrated writers, astonishing geniuses, novels, romances, poems, histories, and dense political economy quartos, which, compared with *Mrs. Leicester's School*, will be remembered as often and prized as highly as Wilkie's and Glover's *Epics*, and Lord Bolingbroke's *Philosophics* compared with *Robinson Crusoe.*"

But a not unimportant question is, What have the little folk thought? The answer is incontrovertible. The first edition sold out immediately, and four more were called for in the course of five years. It has continued in fair demand ever since, though there have not been anything like so many recent reprints as of the *Tales from Shakespeare*. It is one of those children's books which to reopen in afterlife is like revisiting some sunny old garden, some favorite haunt of childhood, where every nook and cranny seems familiar and calls up a thousand pleasant memories.

Mrs. Leicester's School was published at Godwin's Juvenile Library, Skinner street, Christmas, 1808; and, stimulated by its immediate success and by Godwin's encouragement, Mary once more set to work, this time to try her hand in verse.

But meanwhile came the domestic upset of a removal; nay, of two. The landlord of the rooms in Mitre Court Buildings wanted them for himself, and so the Lambs had to quit. March 28, 1809, Charles writes to Manning: "While I think on it let me tell you we are moved. Don't come any more to Mitre Court Buildings. We are at 34 Southampton Buildings, Chancery Lane, and shall be here till about the end of May; then we remove to No. 4 Inner Temple Lane, where I mean to live and die, for I have such a horror of moving that I would not take a benefice from the king if I was not indulged with non-residence. What a dislocation of comfort is comprised in that word 'moving.' Such a heap of little nasty things, after you think all is got into the cart: old dredging-boxes, worn-out brushes, gallipots, vials, things that it is impossible the most necessitous person can ever want, but which the women who preside on these occasions will not leave behind if it was to save your soul. They'd keep the cart ten minutes to stow in dirty pipes and broken matches, to show their economy. Then you can find nothing you want for many days after you get into your new lodgings. You must comb your hair with your fingers, wash your hands without soap, go about in dirty gaiters. Were I

Diogenes I would not move out of a kilderkin into a hogshead, though the first had had nothing but small beer in it, and the second reeked claret."

The unwonted stress of continuous literary work and turmoil and fatigue of a double removal produced the effect that might have been anticipated on Mary. In June (1809) Lamb wrote to Coleridge of his change "to more commodious quarters. I have two rooms on the third floor," he continues, "and five rooms above, with an inner staircase to myself, new painted, and all for £30 a year! I came into them on Saturday week, and on Monday following Mary was taken ill with the fatigue of moving; and affected, I believe, by the novelty of the house, she could not sleep, and I am left alone with a maid quite a stranger to me, and she has a month or two's sad distraction to go through. What sad, large pieces it cuts out of life!—out of *her* life, who is getting rather old; and we may not have many years to live together. I am weaker, and bear it worse than I ever did. But I hope we shall be comfortable by and by. The rooms are delicious, and the best look backwards into Hare Court, where there is a pump always going. Just now it is dry. Hare Court trees come in at the window, so that 'tis like living in a garden. I try to persuade myself it is much pleasanter than Mitre Court; but alas! the household gods are slow to come in a new mansion. They are in their infancy to me; I do not feel them yet; no hearth has blazed to them yet. How I hate and dread new places! . . . Let me hear from some of you, for I am desolate. I shall have to send you, in a week or two, two volumes of juvenile poetry done by Mary and me within the last six months, and that tale in prose which Wordsworth so much liked, which was published at Christmas with nine others by us, and has reached a second edition. There's for you! We have almost worked ourselves out of child's work, and I don't know what to do. . . . Our little poems are but humble, but they have no name. You must read them, remembering they were task-work; and perhaps you will admire the number of subjects, all of children, picked out by an old bachelor and an old maid. Many parents would not have found so many."

Lamb left his friends to guess which were his and which Mary's. Were it a question of their prose the task were easy. The brother's "witty delicacy" of style, the gentle irony under which was hid his deep wisdom, the frolicsome, fantastic humors that often veiled his tenderness, are individual, unique. But in verse, and especially in a little volume of "task-work," those fragments of Mary's which he quotes in his letters show them to have been more similar and equal. It is certain only that *The Three Friends, Queen Oriana's Dream,* and the lines *To a River in which a Child was Drowned,* were his, and that his total share was "one-third in quantity of the whole;" also that *The Two Boys* (reprinted by Lamb in his *Detached Thoughts on Books and Reading*), *David in the Cave of Adullam,* and *The First Tooth,* are certainly Mary's. Through all there breathes a sweet and wise spirit; but some-times, and no doubt on Mary's part, the desire to enforce a moral is too obtrusive, and the teaching too direct, though always it is of a high and generous kind, never pragmatic and pharisaic, after the manner of Dr. Watts. That difficult art of artlessness and perfect simplicity, as in Blake's *Songs of Innocence,* which a child's mind demands and a mature mind loves, is rarely attained. Yet I think *The Beasts in the Tower, Crumbs to the Birds, Motes in the Sunbeam, The Coffee Slips, The Broken Doll, The Books and the Sparrow, Blind-ness, The Two Boys,* and others not a few, must have been favorites in many a nursery.

The Text—in which a self-satisfied little gentleman who listens to and remembers all the sermon is contrasted, much to his disadvantage, with his sister, who did not hear a word, because her heart was full of affectionate longing to make up a quarrel they had had outside the church-door — is very pretty in a moral if not in a musical point of view. This and the three examples which I subjoin were certainly Mary's. The lullaby calls up a picture of her as a sad child nursing her little Charles, though he was no orphan : —

NURSING.

O hush, my little baby brother ;
Sleep, my little baby brother ;
   Sleep, my love, upon my knee.
What though, dear child, we've lost our mother ?
   That can never trouble thee.

You are but ten weeks old to-morrow ;
   What can *you* know of our loss ?
The house is full enough of sorrow.
   Little baby, don't be cross.

Peace ! cry not so, my dearest love ;
   Hush, my baby-bird, lie still ;
He's quiet now, he does not move ;
   Fast asleep is little Will.

My only solace, only joy,
   Since the sad day I lost my mother,
Is nursing her own Willy boy,
   My little orphan brother.

The gentle raillery of the next seems equally characteristic of Mary : —

FEIGNED COURAGE.

Horatio, of ideal courage vain,
Was flourishing in air his father's cane;
And, as the fumes of valor swelled his pate,
Now thought himself *this* hero, and now *that :*
"And now," he cried, "I will Achilles be;
My sword I brandish; see the Trojans flee!
Now I'll be Hector when his angry blade
A lane through heaps of slaughtered Grecians made;
And now, by deeds still braver, I'll evince
I am no less than Edward the Black Prince :
Give way, ye coward French!"—As thus he spoke,
And aimed in fancy a sufficient stroke
To fix the fate of Cressy or Poictiers
(The Muse relates the hero's fate with tears),
He struck his milk-white hand against a nail,
Sees his own blood and feels his courage fail.
Ah! where is now that boasted valor flown,
That in the tented field so late was shown?
Achilles weeps, great Hector hangs the head,
And the Black Prince goes whimpering to bed!

The last is so pretty a little song it deserves to be fitted with an appropriate melody :—

CRUMBS TO THE BIRDS.

A bird appears a thoughtless thing;
He's ever living on the wing,
And keeps up such a caroling,
That little else to do but sing
　　A man would guess had he.

No doubt he has his little cares,
And very hard he often fares,
The which so patiently he bears,
That, listening to those cheerful airs,
    Who knows but he may be
In want of his next meal of seeds?
I think for *that* his sweet song pleads.
If so, his pretty art succeeds;
I'll scatter there among the weeds
    All the small crumbs I see.

Poetry for Children, Entirely Original, by the Author of Mrs. Leicester's School, as the title-page runs, was published in the summer of 1809, and the whole of the first edition sold off rapidly; but instead of being reprinted entire, selections from it only — twenty-six out of the eighty-four pieces — were incorporated, by a schoolmaster of the name of Mylius, in two books, called *The First Book of Poetry* and *The Poetical Class Book,* issued from the same Juvenile Library in 1810. These went through many editions, but ultimately dropped quite out of sight, as the original work had already done. Writing to Bernard Barton in 1827, Lamb says: "One likes to have one copy of everything one does. I neglected to keep one of *Poetry for Children,* the joint production of Mary and me, and it is not to be had for love or money." Fifty years later such specimens of these poems as could be gathered from the Mylius collections

and from Lamb's own works were republished
by Mr. W. Carew Hazlitt, and also by Richard
Herne Shepherd, when at last, in 1877, there
came to hand from Australia a copy of the original edition; it had been purchased at a sale of
books and furniture at Plymouth, in 1866, and
thence carried to Adelaide. It was reprinted
entire by Mr. Shepherd (Chatto and Windus,
1878), with a preface from which the foregoing
details have been gathered. A New England
publisher early descried the worth of the *Poetry
for Children*, for it was reprinted in Boston —
eighty-one pieces, at least, out of the eighty-
four — in 1812. A copy of this American edition also has recently come to light.

This was Mary's last literary undertaking in
book form; but there is reason to think she
wrote occasional articles for periodicals for some
years longer. One such, at any rate, on *Needlework*, written in 1814, is mentioned by Crabb
Robinson, of which more hereafter.

CHAPTER XI.

1808-13. — Æt. 44-49.

HAZLITT and his bride had, for the present,
settled down in Sara's cottage at Winterslow;
so Mary continued to send them every now and
then a pretty budget of gossip: —

"DEC. 10, 1808.

"I hear of you from your brother, but you do
not write yourself, nor does Hazlitt. I beg that
one or both of you will amend this fault as
speedily as possible, for I am very anxious to
hear of your health. . . . You cannot think
how very much we miss you and H. of a
Wednesday evening. All the glory of the
night, I may say, is at an end. Phillips makes
his jokes, and there is none to applaud him;
Rickman argues, and there is no one to oppose
him. The worst miss of all to me is that, when
we are in the dismals, there is now no hope of
relief from any quarter whatsoever. Hazlitt
was most brilliant, most ornamental as a

Wednesday man; but he was a more useful
one on common days, when he dropt in after a
quarrel or a fit of the glooms. The Sheffington
is quite out now, my brother having got drunk
with claret and Tom Sheridan. This visit and
the occasion of it is a profound secret, and
therefore I tell it to nobody but you and Mrs.
Reynolds. Through the medium of Wroughton there came an invitation and proposal from
T. S. that C. L. should write some scenes in a
speaking pantomime, the other parts of which
Tom now, and his father formerly, have manu-
factured between them. So, in the Christmas
holidays, my brother and his two great associ-
ates, we expect, will be all three damned
together,—that is, I mean, if Charles' share,
which is done and sent in, is accepted.

"I left this unfinished yesterday in the hope
that my brother would have done it for me; his
reason for refusing me was no 'exquisite reason;' for it was because he must write a letter
to Manning in three or four weeks, and therefore he could not always be writing letters, he
said. I wanted him to tell your husband about
a great work which Godwin is going to publish
[an *Essay on Sepulchres*], to enlighten the world
once more, and I shall not be able to make out
what it is. He (Godwin) took his usual walk
one evening, a fortnight since, to the end of

Hatton Garden and back again. During that walk a thought came into his mind which he instantly set down and improved upon till he brought it, in seven or eight days, into the compass of a reasonable-sized pamphlet : to propose a subscription to all well-disposed people to raise a certain sum of money, to be expended in the care of a cheap monument for the former and the future great dead men — the monument to be a white cross with a wooden slab at the end, telling their names and qualifications ; this wooden slab and white cross to be perpetuated to the end of time. To survive the fall of empires and the destruction of cities by means of a map which was, in case of an insurrection among the people, or any other cause by which a city or country may be destroyed, to be carefully preserved, and then when things got again into their usual order, the white-cross wooden-slab makers were to go to work again and set them in their former places. This, as nearly as I can tell you, is the sum and substance of it ; but it is written remarkably well, in his very best manner, for the proposal (which seems to me very like throwing salt on a sparrow's tail to catch him) occupies but half a page, which is followed by very fine writing on the benefits he conjectures would follow if it were done. Very excellent thoughts on death and on our feelings

8

concerning dead friends, and the advantages an old country has over a new one, even in the slender memorials we have of great men who once flourished.

"Charles is come home and wants his dinner, and so the dead men must be no more thought on. Tell us how you go on and how you like Winterslow and winter evenings. Noales [Knowles] has not got back again, but he is in better spirits. John Hazlitt was here on Wednesday, very sober. Our love to Hazlitt.

"There came this morning a printed prospectus from S. T. Coleridge, Grasmere, of a weekly paper to be called *The Friend;* a flaming prospectus — I have no time to give the heads of it; to commence first Saturday in January. There came also a notice of a turkey from Mr. Clarkson, which I am more sanguine in expecting the accomplishment of than I am of Coleridge's prophecy."

A few weeks after the date of this letter Sara had a little son. He lived but six months; just enough for his father's restless, dissatisfied heart to taste for once the sweetness of a tie unalloyed with any bitterness, and the memory of it never faded out. There is a pathetic allusion in one of his latest essays to a visit to the neglected spot where the baby was laid, and where still, "as the nettles wave in a corner of

the churchyard over his little grave, the welcome breeze helps to refresh me and ease the
tightness at my breast."

In March of this year, too, died one of the
most conspicuous members of Lamb's circle,
Thomas Holcroft; dear to Godwin, but not,
perhaps, a great favorite with the Lambs. He
was too dogmatic and disputatious—a man
who would pull you up at every turn for a
definition, which, as Coleridge said, was like
setting up perpetual turnpikes along the road
to truth. Hazlitt undertook to write his life.

The visit to Winterslow which had been so
often talked of before Sara's marriage was
again under discussion, and on June 2d, Mary,
full of thoughtful consideration for her hosts
that were to be, writes jointly with Martin
Burney :—

"You may write to Hazlitt that I will *certainly*
go to Winterslow, as my father has agreed to
give me £5 to bear my expenses, and has given
leave that I may stop till that is spent, leaving
enough to defray my carriage on 14th July.

"So far Martin has written, and further than
that I can give you no intelligence, for I do
not yet know Phillips' intentions ; nor can I tell
the exact time when we can come ; nor can I
positively say we shall come at all, for we have
scruples of conscience about there being so

many of us. Martin says if you can borrow a blanket or two he can sleep on the floor without either bed or mattress, which would save his expenses at the Hut ; for if Phillips breakfasts there he must do so too, which would swallow up all his money ; and he and I have calculated that if he has no inn expenses he may well spare that money to give you for a part of his roast beef. We can spare you also just five pounds. You are not to say this to Hazlitt, lest his delicacy should be alarmed; but I tell you what Martin and I have planned, that if you happen to be empty-pursed at this time, you may think it as well to make him up a bed in the best kitchen. I think it very probable that Phillips will come, and if you do not like such a crowd of us, for they both talk of staying a whole month, tell me so, and we will put off our visit till next summer.

"Thank you very much for the good work you have done for me. Mrs. Stoddart also thanks you for the gloves. How often must I tell you never to do any needlework for anybody but me ? . . .

" I cannot write any more, for we have got a noble life of Lord Nelson, lent us for a short time by my poor relation the bookbinder, and I want to read as much of it as I can."

The death of the baby and one of Mary's

severe attacks of illness combined to postpone the visit till autumn; but when it did come to pass it completely restored her, and left lasting remembrance of its pleasures both with hosts and guests. Charles tells Coleridge (Oct. 30): "The journey has been of infinite service to Mary. We have had nothing but sunshiny days, and daily walks from eight to twenty miles a day. Have seen Wilton, Salisbury, Stonehenge, etc. Her illness lasted just six weeks; it left her weak, but the country has made us whole."

And Mary herself wrote to Sara (Nov. 7): "The dear, quiet, lazy, delicious month we spent with you is remembered by me with such regret that I feel quite discontented and Winterslow-sick. I assure you I never passed such a pleasant time in the country in my life, both in the house and out of it, — the card-playing quarrels, and a few gaspings for breath after your swift footsteps up the high hills, excepted; and those drawbacks are not unpleasant in the recollection. We have got some salt butter to make our toast seem like yours, and we have tried to eat meat suppers, but that would not do, for we left our appetites behind us; and the dry loaf which offended you now comes in at night unaccompanied; but, sorry I am to add, it is soon followed by the pipe and the gin-bottle. We smoked the very first night of our arrival.

"Great news! I have just been interrupted by Mr. Dawe, who comes to tell me he was yesterday elected an Academician. He said none of his own friends voted for him; he has got it by strangers, who were pleased with his picture of Mrs. White. Charles says he does not believe Northcote ever voted for the admission of any one. Though a very cold day, Dawe was in a prodigious sweat for joy at his good fortune.

"More great news! My beautiful green curtains were put up yesterday, and all the doors listed with green baize, and four new boards put to the coal-hole, and fastening hasps put to the window, and my dyed Manning silk cut out.

"Yesterday was an eventful day, for yesterday, too, Martin Burney was to be examined by Lord Eldon, previous to his being admitted as an attorney; but he has not been here yet to announce his success.

"I carried the baby-caps to Mrs. John Hazlitt. She was much pleased and vastly thankful. Mr. H. got fifty-four guineas at Rochester, and has now several pictures in hand.

"I am going to tell you a secret, for ———— says she would be sorry to have it talked of. One night ———— came home from the alehouse, bringing with him a great, rough, illlooking fellow, whom he introduced to ————

as Mr. Brown, a gentleman he had hired as a mad-keeper, to take care of him at forty pounds a year, being ten pounds under the usual price for keepers, which sum Mr. Brown had agreed to remit out of pure friendship. It was with great difficulty and by threatening to call in the aid of a watchman and constables that——could prevail on Mr. Brown to leave the house.

"We had a good chearful meeting on Wednesday; much talk of Winterslow, its woods and its nice sunflowers. I did not so much like Phillips at Winterslow as I now like him for having been with us at Winterslow. We roasted the last of his 'beech of oily nut prolific' on Friday at the Captain's. Nurse is now established in Paradise, *alias* the incurable ward of Westminster Hospital. I have seen her sitting in most superb state, surrounded by her seven incurable companions. They call each other ladies. Nurse looks as if she would be considered as the first lady in the ward; only one seemed like to rival her in dignity.

"A man in the India House has resigned, by which Charles will get twenty pounds a year, and White has prevailed upon him to write some more lottery puffs. If that ends in smoke the twenty pounds is a sure card, and has made us very joyful. I continue very well, and return you my sincere thanks for my good health and improved looks, which have almost made Mrs. Godwin die with envy ; she longs to come to Winterslow as much as the spiteful elder sister did to go to the well for a gift to spit diamonds.

"Jane and I have agreed to boil a round of beef for your suppers when you come to town again.   She, Jane, broke two of the Hogarth glasses while we were away, whereat I made a great noise.

"Farewell.   Love to William, and Charles' love and good wishes for the speedy arrival of the *Life of Holcroft* and the bearer thereof. Charles told Mrs. Godwin Hazlitt had found a well in his garden which, water being scarce in your country, would bring him in two hundred a year ; and she came in great haste the next morning to ask me if it were true."

Hazlitt, too, remembered to the end of his life those golden autumn days : "Lamb among the villagers like the most capricious poet Ovid among the Goths ;" the evening walks with him and Mary to look at "the Claude Lorraine skies melting from azure into purple and gold, and to gather mushrooms that sprung up at our feet, to throw into our hashed mutton at supper."

When Lamb called to congratulate Mr. Dawe on his good fortune his housekeeper seemed embarrassed, owned that her master was alone, but ushered in the visitor with reluctance. For why? "At his easel stood D., with an immense spread of canvas before him, and by his side — a live goose. Under the rose he informed me that he had undertaken to paint a transparency for Vauxhall, against an expected visit of the allied sovereigns. I smiled at an engagement so derogatory to his new-born honors; but a contempt of small gains was never one of D.'s foibles. My eyes beheld crude forms of warriors, kings rising under his brush upon this interminable stretch of cloth. The Volga, the Don, the Dnieper were there, or their representative river gods, and Father Thames clubbed urns with the Vistula. Glory, with her dazzling eagle, was not absent, nor Fame, nor Victory. The shade of Rubens might have evoked the mighty allegories. But what was the goose? He was evidently sitting for a something. D. at last informed me that he could not introduce the Royal Thames without his *swans;* that he had inquired the price of a live swan, and it being more than he was prepared to give for it, he had bargained with the poulterer for the *next thing to it,* adding significantly that it would do to roast after it had served its turn to paint swans by." (Lamb's *Recollections of a Royal Academician.*)

The following year the visit to Winterslow was repeated, but not with the same happy results. In a letter written during his stay to Mr. Basil Montague, Charles says: "My head has received such a shock by an all-night journey on the top of the coach that I shall have enough to do to nurse it into its natural pace before I go home. I must devote myself to imbecility; I must be gloriously useless while I stay here. The city of Salisbury is full of weeping and wailing. The bank has stopped payment, and everybody in the town kept money at it, or has got some of its notes. Some have lost all they had in the world. It is the next thing to seeing a city with the plague within its walls; and I do suppose it to be the unhappiest county in England—this, where I am making holiday. We purpose setting out for Oxford Tuesday fortnight, and coming thereby home. But no more night-travelling; my head is sore (understand it of the inside) with that deduction from my natural rest which I suffered coming down. Neither Mary nor I can spare a morsel of our rest; it is incumbent on us to be misers of it."

The visit to Oxford was paid, Hazlitt accompanying them and much enhancing the enjoyment of it, especially of a visit to the picture gallery at Blenheim. "But our pleasant excur-

sion has ended sadly for one of us," he tells
Hazlitt on his return. "My sister got home
very well (I was very ill on the journey), and
continued so till Monday night, when her complaint came on, and she is now absent from
home. I think I shall be mad if I take any
more journeys, with two experiences against it.
I have lost all wish for sights."

It was a long attack; at the end of October
Mary was still "very weak and low-spirited,"
and there were domestic misadventures not calculated to improve matters.

"We are in a pickle," says Charles to Wordsworth. "Mary, from her affectation of physi-
ognomy, has hired a stupid, big, country wench,
who looked honest, as she thought, and has
been doing her work some days, but without
eating; and now it comes out that she was ill
when she came, with lifting her mother about
(who is now with God) when she was dying,
and with riding up from Norfolk four days and
nights in the wagon, and now she lies in her
bed, a dead weight upon our humanity, incapable
of getting up, refusing to go to a hospital, having nobody in town but a poor asthmatic uncle,
and she seems to have made up her mind to
take her flight to Heaven from our bed. Oh,
for the little wheelbarrow which trundled the
hunchback from door to door to try the various

charities of different professions of mankind! Here's her uncle just crawled up; he is far liker death than she. In this perplexity such topics as Spanish papers and Monkhouses sink into insignificance. What shall we do?"

The perplexity seems to have cleared itself up somehow speedily, for in a week's time Mary herself wrote to Mrs. Hazlitt, not very cheerfully, but with no allusion to this particular disaster:—

"Nov. 30, 1810.

"I have taken a large sheet of paper, as if I were going to write a long letter; but that is by no means my intention, for I have only time to write three lines, to notify what I ought to have done the moment I received your welcome letter; namely, that I shall be very much joyed to see you. Every morning lately I have been expecting to see you drop in, even before your letter came; and I have been setting my wits to work to think how to make you as comfortable as the nature of our inhospitable habits will admit. I must work while you are here, and I have been slaving very hard to get through with something before you come, that I may be quite in the way of it, and not teize you with complaints all day that I do not know what to do.

"I am very sorry to hear of your mischance.

Mrs. Rickman has just buried her youngest child. I am glad I am an old maid, for you see there is nothing but misfortunes in the marriage state. Charles was drunk last night and drunk the night before, which night before was at Godwin's, where we went, at a short summons from Mr. G., to play a solitary rubber, which was interrupted by the entrance of Mr. and little Mrs. Liston; and after them came Henry Robinson, who is now domesticated at Mr. Godwin's fire-side, and likely to become a formidable rival to Tommy Turner. We finished there at twelve o'clock, Charles and Liston brim-full of gin-and-water and snuff, after which Henry Robinson spent a long evening by our fire-side at home, and there was much gin-and-water drunk, albeit only one of the party partook of it, and H. R. professed himself highly indebted to Charles for the useful information he gave him on sundry matters of taste and imagination, even after Charles could not speak plain for tipsiness. But still he swallowed the flattery and the spirits as savorily as Robinson did his cold water.

"Last night was to be a night, but it was not. There was a certain son of one of Martin's employers, one young Mr. Blake, to do whom honor Mrs. Burney brought forth, first rum, then a single bottle of champaine, long

kept in her secret hoard; then two bottles of
her best currant wine, which she keeps for Mrs.
Rickman, came out; and Charles partook liber-
ally of all these beverages, while Mr. Young
Blake and Mr. Ireton talked of high matters,
such as the merits of the Whip Club, and the
merits of red and white champaine. Do I spell
that last word right? Rickman was not there,
so Ireton had it all his own way.

"The alternating Wednesdays will chop off
one day in the week from your jolly days, and I
do not know how we shall make it up to you,
but I will contrive the best I can. Phillips
comes again pretty regularly, to the great joy
of Mrs. Reynolds. Once more she hears the
well-loved sounds of 'How do you do, Mrs.
Reynolds?' and 'How does Miss Chambers
do?'

"I have spun out my three lines amazingly;
now for family news. Your brother's little
twins are not dead, but Mrs. John Hazlitt and
her baby may be for anything I know to the
contrary, for I have not been there for a prodigious long time. Mrs. Holcroft still goes
about from Nicholson to Tuthill, and Tuthill to
Godwin, and from Godwin to Nicholson, to consult on the publication or no publication of the
life of the good man, her husband. It is called
The Life Everlasting. How does that same life

go on in your parts? Good bye; God bless you. I shall be glad to see you when you come this way.

"I am going in great haste to see Mrs. Clarkson, for I must get back to dinner, which I have hardly time to do. I wish that dear, good, amiable woman would go out of town. I thought she was clean gone, and yesterday there was a consultation of physicians held at her house, to see if they could keep her among them here a few weeks longer."

The concluding volumes of this same *Life Everlasting* remained unprinted somewhere in a damp hamper, Mr. Carew Hazlitt tells us; for, in truth, the admirable fragment of autobiography Holcroft dictated on his death-bed contained the cream of the matter, and was all the public cared to listen to.

Mary continuing "in a feeble and tottering condition," Charles found it needful to make a decisive stand on her behalf against the exhaustion and excitement of incessant company, and especially against the disturbed rest, which resulted from sharing her room with a guest:—

"Nov. 28, 1810.

"Mary has been very ill indeed since you saw her," he wrote to Hazlitt; "as ill as she can be to remain at home. But she is a good deal better now, owing to a very careful regimen. She drinks nothing but water, and never goes out; she does not even go to the Captain's. Her indisposition has been ever since that night you left town, the night Miss Wordsworth came. Her coming, and that d——d Mrs. Godwin coming and staying so late that night, so overset her that she lay broad awake all that night, and it was by a miracle that she escaped a very bad illness, which I thoroughly expected. I have made up my mind that she shall never have any one in the house again with her, and that no one shall sleep with her, not even for a night; for it is a very serious thing to be always living with a kind of fever upon her; and therefore I am sure you will take it in good part if I say that if Mrs. Hazlitt comes to town at any time, however glad we shall be to see her in the day-time, I cannot ask her to spend a night under our roof. Some decision we must come to; for the harassing fever that we have both been in, owing to Miss Wordsworth's coming, is not to be borne, and I would rather be dead than so alive. However, owing to a regimen and medicines which Tuthill has given her, who very kindly volunteered the care of her, she is a great deal quieter, though too much harassed by company, who cannot or will not see how late hours and society teaze her.

The next letter to Sara is a cheerful one, as the occasion demanded. It is also the last to her that has been preserved, probably the last that was written; for, a few months later, Hazlitt fairly launched himself on a literary career in London, and took up his abode next door to Jeremy Bentham, at 19 York street, Westminster, once Milton's house: —

"OCT. 2, 1811.

"I have been a long time anxiously expecting the happy news that I have just received. I address you because, as the letter has been lying some days at the India House, I hope you are able to sit up and read my congratulations on the little live boy you have been so many years wishing for. As we old women say, 'May he live to be a great comfort to you!' I never knew an event of the kind that gave me so much pleasure as the little long-looked-for-come-at-last's arrival; and I rejoice to hear his honor has begun to suck. The word was not distinctly written, and I was a long time making out the solemn fact. I hope to hear from you soon, for I am anxious to know if your nursing labors are attended with any difficulties. I wish you a happy *getting-up* and a merry christening!

"Charles sends his love; perhaps, though,

he will write a scrap to Hazlitt at the end. He is now looking over me. He is always in my way, for he has had a month's holiday at home. But I am happy to say they end on Monday, when mine begin, for I am going to pass a week at Richmond with Mrs. Burney. She has been dying, but she went to the Isle of Wight and recovered once more, and she is finishing her recovery at Richmond. When there, I mean to read novels and play at piquet all day long."

"My blessing and Heaven's be upon him," added Charles, "and make him like his father, with something a better temper and a smoother head of hair, and then all the men and women must love him." . . .

CHAPTER XII.

An Essay on Needlework.

TOWARDS the end of 1814 Crabb Robinson called on Mary Lamb and found her suffering from great fatigue after writing an article on needlework for the *British Lady's Magazine*, which was just about to start on a higher basis than its predecessors. It undertook to provide something better than the usual fashion-plates, silly tales and sillier verses then generally thought suitable for women; and, to judge by the early numbers, the editor kept the promise of his introductory address, and deserved a longer lease of life for his magazine than it obtained.

Mary's little essay appeared in the number for April, 1815, and is on many accounts interesting. It contains several autobiographic touches; it is the only known instance in which she has addressed herself to full-grown readers, and it is sagacious and far-seeing. For Mary does not treat of needlework as an art, but as a

factor in social life. She pleads both for the
sake of the bodily welfare of the many thousands of women who have to earn their bread
by it, and of the mental well-being of those
who have not so to do; that it should be
regarded, like any other mechanical art, as a
thing to be done for hire; and that what a
woman· *does* work at should be real work —
something, that is, which yields a return either
of mental or of pecuniary profit. She also
exposes the fallacy of the time-honored maxim,
"A penny saved is a penny earned," by the ruth-
less logic of experience. But the reader shall
judge for himself; the *Magazine* has become so
rare a book that I will here subjoin the little
essay in full: —

ON NEEDLEWORK.

"MR. EDITOR:

"In early life I passed eleven years in the
exercise of my needle for a livelihood. Will
you allow me to address your readers, among
whom might perhaps be found some of the kind
patronesses of my former humble labors, on a
subject widely connected with female life — the
state of needlework in this country?

"To lighten the heavy burthen which many
ladies impose upon themselves is one object
which I have in view; but I confess my strong-

est motive is to excite attention towards the industrious sisterhood to which I once belonged.

"From books I have been informed of the fact upon which *The British Lady's Magazine* chiefly founds its pretensions; namely, that women have of late been rapidly advancing in intellectual improvement. Much may have been gained in this way, indirectly, for that class of females for whom I wish to plead. Needlework and intellectual improvement are naturally in a state of warfare. But I am afraid the root of evil has not, as yet, been struck at. Workwomen of every description were never in so much distress for want of employment.

"Among the present circle of my acquaintance I am proud to rank many that may truly be called respectable; nor do the female part of them in their mental attainments at all disprove the prevailing opinion of that intellectual progression which you have taken as the basis of your work; yet I affirm that I know not a single family where there is not some essential drawback to its comfort, which may be traced to needlework *done at home*, as the phrase is, for all needlework performed in a family by some of its own members, and for which no remuneration in money is received or expected.

"In money alone, did I say? I would appeal to all the fair votaries of voluntary housewifery whether, in the matter of conscience, any one of them ever thought she had done as much needlework as she ought to have done. Even fancy work, the fairest of the tribe! How delightful the arrangement of her materials! The fixing upon her happiest pattern, how pleasing an anxiety! How cheerful the commencement of the labor she enjoys! But that lady must be a true lover of the art, and so industrious a pursuer of a predetermined purpose, that it were pity her energy should not have been directed to some wiser end, who can affirm she neither feels weariness during the execution of a fancy piece, nor takes more time than she had calculated for the performance.

"Is it too bold an attempt to persuade your readers that it would prove an incalculable addition to general happiness and the domestic comfort of both sexes, if needlework were never practiced but for a remuneration in money? As nearly, however, as this desirable thing can be effected, so much more nearly will woman be upon an equality with men as far as respects the mere enjoyment of life. As far as that goes, I believe it is every woman's opinion that the condition of men is far superior to her own.

" 'They can do what they like,' we say. Do not these words generally mean they have time to seek out whatever amusements suit their tastes? We dare not tell them we have no time to do this; for if they should ask in what manner we dispose of our time we should blush to enter upon a detail of the minutiæ which compose the sum of a woman's daily employment. Nay, many a lady, who allows not herself one-quarter of an hour's positive leisure during her waking hours, considers her own husband as the most industrious of men if he steadily pursue his occupation till the hour of dinner, and will be perpetually lamenting her own idleness.

"*Real business* and *real leisure* make up the portions of men's time, — two sources of happiness which we certainly partake of in a very inferior degree. To the execution of employments in which the faculties of the body or mind are called into busy action there must be a consoling importance attached, which feminine duties (that generic term for all our business) cannot aspire to.

"In the most meritorious discharges of those duties the highest praise we can aim at is to be accounted the helpmates of *man;* who, in return for all he does for us, expects, and justly expects, us to do all in our power to soften and sweeten life.

"In how many ways is a good woman employed in thought or action through the day, that her *good man* may be enabled to feel his leisure hours *real*, *substantial holiday*, and perfect respite from the cares of business! Not the least part to be done to accomplish this end is to fit herself to become a conversational companion; that is to say, she has to study and understand the subjects on which he loves to talk. This part of our duty, if strictly performed, will be found by far our hardest part. The disadvantages we labor under from an education differing from a manly one make the hours in which we *sit and do nothing* in men's company too often anything but a relaxation; although as to pleasure and instruction, time so passed may be esteemed more or less delightful.

"To make a man's home so desirable a place as to preclude his having a wish to pass his leisure hours at any fire-side in preference to his own, I should humbly take to be the sum and substance of woman's domestic ambition. I would appeal to our British ladies, who are generally allowed to be the most jealous and successful of all women in the pursuit of this object; I would appeal to them who have been most successful in the performance of this laudable service, in behalf of father, son, husband or brother, whether an anxious desire to perform this duty well is not attended with enough of *mental* exertion, at least, to incline them to the opinion that women may be more properly ranked among the contributors to than the partakers of the undisturbed relaxation of men.

"If a family be so well ordered that the master is never called in to its direction, and yet he perceives comfort and economy well attended to, the mistress of that family (especially if children form a part of it) has, I apprehend, as large a share of womanly employment as ought to satisfy her own sense of duty; even though the needle-book and thread-case were quite laid aside, and she cheerfully contributed her part to the slender gains of the corset-maker, the milliner, the dressmaker, the plain worker, the embroidress and all the numerous classifications of females supporting themselves by needlework, that great staple commodity which is alone appropriated to the self-supporting part of our sex.

"Much has been said and written on the subject of men engrossing to themselves every occupation and calling. After many years of observation and reflection I am obliged to acquiesce in the notion that it cannot well be ordered otherwise.

"If, at the birth of girls, it were possible to foresee in what cases it would be their fortune to pass a single life, we should soon find trades

wrested from their present occupiers and transferred to the exclusive possession of our sex.
The whole mechanical business of copying writings in the law department, for instance, might
very soon be transferred with advantage to the
poorer sort of women, who, with very little
teaching, would soon beat their rivals of the
other sex in facility and neatness. The parents
of female children who were known to be des-
tined from their birth to maintain themselves
through the whole course of their lives, with
like certainty as their sons are, would feel it a
duty incumbent on themselves to strengthen
the minds and even the bodily constitutions of
their girls so circumstanced, by an education
which, without affronting the preconceived habits of society, might enable them to follow some
occupation now considered above the capacity,
or too robust for the constitution, of our sex.
Plenty of resources would then lie open for
single women to obtain an independent livelihood, when every parent would be upon the
alert to encroach upon some employment now
engrossed by men, for such of their daughters
as would then be exactly in the same predica-
ment as their sons now are. Who, for instance,
would lay by money to set up his sons in trade,
give premiums, and in part maintain them
through a long apprenticeship; or, which men

of moderate incomes frequently do, strain every nerve in order to bring them up to a learned profession ; if it were in a very high degree probable that, by the time they were twenty years of age, they would be taken from this trade or profession, and maintained during the remainder of their lives by the *person whom they should marry?* Yet this is precisely the situation in which every parent, whose income does not very much exceed the moderate, is placed with respect to his daughters.

"Even where boys have gone through a laborious education, superinducing habits of steady attention accompanied with the entire conviction that the business which they learn is to be the source of their future distinction, may it not be affirmed that the persevering industry required to accomplish this desirable end causes many a hard struggle in the minds of young men, even of the most hopeful disposition ? What, then, must be the disadvantages under which a very young woman is placed who is required to learn a trade, from which she can never expect to reap any profit, but at the expense of losing that place in society to the possession of which she may reasonably look forward, inasmuch as it is by far the most *common lot*, namely, the condition of a *happy* English wife?

"As I desire to offer nothing to the consider-

ation of your readers but what, at least as far as
my own observation goes, I consider as truths
confirmed by experience, I will only say that,
were I to follow the bent of my own speculative
opinion, I should be inclined to persuade every
female over whom I hope to have any influence
to contribute all the assistance in her power to
those of her own sex who may need it, in the
employments they at present occupy, rather than
to force them into situations now filled wholly
by men.   With the mere exception of the profits
which they have a right to derive by their needle,
I would take nothing from the industry of man
which he already possesses.

"'A penny saved is a penny earned,' is a
maxim not true unless the penny be saved in the
same time in which it might have been earned.
I, who have known what it is to work for *money
earned*, have since had much experience in working for *money saved;* and I consider, from the
closest calculation I can make, that a *penny saved*
in that way bears about a true proportion to a
farthing earned.   I am no advocate for women
who do not depend on themselves for subsistence,
proposing to themselves to *earn money.*   My
reasons for thinking it not advisable are too
numerous to state — reasons deduced from authentic facts and strict observations on domestic
life in its various shades of comfort.   But if the

females of a family *nominally* supported by the
other sex find it necessary to add something to
the common stock, why not endeavor to do
something by which they may produce money
in its true shape?

"It would be an excellent plan, attended with
very little trouble, to calculate every evening
how much money has been saved by needlework
done in the family, and compare the result with
the daily portion of the yearly income. Nor
would it be amiss to make a memorandum of
the time passed in this way, adding also a guess
as to what share it has taken up in the thoughts
and conversation. This would be an easy mode
of forming a true notion and getting at the
exact worth of this species of *home* industry,
and perhaps might place it in a different light
from any in which it has hitherto been the fashion to consider it.

"Needlework taken up as an amusement may
not be altogether unamusing. We are all pretty
good judges of what entertains ourselves, but
it is not so easy to pronounce upon what may
contribute to the entertainment of others. At
all events, let us not confuse the motives of
economy with those of simple pastime. If *saving* be no object, and long habits have rendered
needlework so delightful an avocation that we
cannot think of relinquishing it, there are the

good old contrivances in which our grand-dames were wont to beguile and lose their time — knitting, knotting, netting, carpet-work, and the like ingenious pursuits — those so often praised but tedious works, which are so long in the operation that purchasing the labor has seldom been thought good economy. Yet by a certain fascination they have been found to chain down the great to a self-imposed slavery, from which they considerately or haughtily excused the needy. These may be esteemed lawful and lady-like amusements. But, if those works more usually denominated useful yield greater satisfaction, it might be a laudable scruple of conscience, and no bad test to herself of her own motive, if a lady who had no absolute need were to give the money so saved to poor needle-women belonging to those branches of employment from which she has borrowed these shares of pleasurable labor.

" SEMPRONIA."

Had Mary lived now she would, perhaps, have spoken a wiser word than has yet been uttered on the urgent question of how best to develop, strengthen, give free and fair scope to that large part of a woman's nature and field of action which are the same in kind as man's, without detriment to the remaining qualities and duties peculiar to her as woman. She told Crabb Robinson that "writing was a most painful occupation, which only necessity could make her attempt; and that she had been learning Latin merely to assist her in acquiring a correct style." But there is no trace of feebleness or confusion in her manner of grasping a subject; no want of Latin nor of anything else to improve her excellent style. She did enough to show that had her brain not been devastated for weeks and latterly for months in every year by an access of madness, she would have left, besides her tales for children, some permanent addition to literature, or given a recognizable impetus to thought. As it was, Mary relinquished all attempt at literary work when an increase in Charles' income released her from the duty of earning; and as her attacks became longer and more frequent, her "fingers grew nervously averse" even to letter-writing.

CHAPTER XIII.

1815–21. — Æt. 51–57.

IN a letter to Southey, dated May 16th, 1815,
Lamb says: "Have you seen Matilda Betham's
Lay of Marie? I think it very delicately pretty
as to sentiment, etc."

Matilda, the daughter of a country clergyman
of ancient lineage (author of learned and laborious *Genealogical Tables,* etc., etc.), was a lady
of many talents and ambitions, especially of the
laudable one, not so common in those days, to
lighten the burthen of a large family of brothers
and sisters by earning her own living. She
went up to London, taught herself miniature
painting, exhibited at Somerset House, gave
Shakespeare readings, wrote a *Biographical
Dictionary of Celebrated Women,* contributed
verses to the magazines, and last, not least, by

her genuine love of knowledge and her warm
and kindly heart, won the cordial liking of many
men of genius, notably of Coleridge, Southey
and the Lambs. When this same *Lay of Marie*
was on the stocks Mary took an earnest interest
in its success, as the following letter prettily
testifies : —

"My brother and myself return you a thousand thanks for your kind communication. We
have read your poem many times over with
increased interest, and very much wish to see
you to tell you how highly we have been pleased
with it. May we beg one favor? I keep the
manuscript in the hope that you will grant it.
It is that either now, or when the whole poem
is completed, you will read it over with us.
When I say 'with *us*,' of course I mean Charles.
I know that you have many judicious friends,
but I have so often known my brother spy out
errors in a manuscript which has passed through
many judicious hands, that I shall not be easy
if you do not permit him to look yours carefully
through with you; and also you *must* allow him
to correct the press for you. If I knew where
to find you I would call upon you. Should you
feel nervous at the idea of meeting Charles in
the capacity of a *severe censor*, give me a line
and I will come to you anywhere and convince
you in five minutes that he is even timid, stam-

9

mers, and can scarcely speak for modesty and fear of giving pain, when he finds himself placed in that kind of office. Shall I appoint a time to see you here when he is from home? I will send him out any time you will name; indeed, I am always naturally alone till four o'clock. If you are nervous about coming, remember I am equally so about the liberty I have taken, and shall be till we meet and laugh off our mutual fears."

"I return you by a careful hand the MSS.," wrote Charles. "Did I not ever love your verses? The domestic half will be a sweet heirloom to have in the family. 'Tis fragrant with cordiality. What friends you must have had, or dreamed of having! and what a widow's cruse of heartiness you have doled among them!"

But as to the correction of the press, that proved a rash suggestion on Mary's part; for the task came at an untoward time, and Charles had to write a whimsical, repentant letter, which must have gone far to atone for his shortcoming: —

"All this while I have been tormenting myself with the thought of having been ungracious to you, and you have been all the while accusing yourself. Let us absolve one another and be quiet. My head is in such a

state from incapacity for business, that I certainly know it to be my duty not to undertake
the veriest trifle in addition. I hardly know
how I can go on. I have tried to get some
redress by explaining my health, but with no
great success. No one can tell how ill I am,
because it does not come out to the exterior
of my face, but lies in my skull, deep and
invisible. I wish I was leprous, and black-
jaundiced skin-over, or that all was as well
within as my cursed looks. You must not
think me worse than I am. I am determined
not to be overset, but to give up business
rather, and get 'em to allow me a trifle for
services past. Oh, that I had been a shoe-
maker, or a baker, or a man of large, independent fortune. Oh, darling laziness! Heaven of
Epicurus! saint's everlasting rest! that I could
drink vast potations of thee through unmeas-
ured eternity. *Otium cum vel sine dignitate.*
Scandalous, dishonorable, any kind of *repose.*
I stand not upon the *dignified sort.* Accursed,
damned desks, trade, commerce, business. Inventions of that old original busy-body, brain-
working Satan — Sabbathless, restless Satan.
A curse relieves; do you ever try it? A
strange letter to write to a lady, but more
honeyed sentences will not distill. I dare not
ask who revises in my stead. I have drawn

you into a scrape, and am ashamed, but I know no remedy. My unwellness must be my apology. God bless you (tho' He curse the India House and fire it *to the ground*), and may no unkind error creep into *Marie*. May all its readers like it as well as I do, and everybody about you like its kind author no worse! Why the devil am I never to have a chance of scribbling my own free thoughts in verse or prose again? Why must I write of tea and drugs, and price goods and bales of indigo? Farewell." . . .

Miss Betham possessed the further merit of having a charming little sister, for such she must surely have been to be the cause and the recipient of such a letter as the following from Mary. Barbara Betham was then fourteen years old:—

"NOVEMBER 2, 1814.

"It is very long since I have met with such an agreeable surprise as the sight of your letter, my kind, kind young friend, afforded me. Such a nice letter as it is, too; and what a pretty hand you write! I congratulate you on this attainment with great pleasure, because I have so often felt the disadvantage of my own wretched handwriting. You wish for London news. I rely upon your sister Ann for gratify-ing you in this respect, yet I have been endeavoring to recollect whom you might have seen here, and what may have happened to them since, and this effort has only brought the image of little Barbara Betham, unconnected with any other person, so strongly before my eyes, that I seem as if I had no other subject to write upon. Now I think I see you with your feet propped upon the fender, your two hands spread out upon your knees — an attitude you always chose when we were in familiar, confidential conversation together — telling me long stories of your own home, where now you say you are 'moping on with the same thing every day,' and which then presented nothing but pleasant recollections to your mind. How well I remember your quiet, steady face bent over your book! One day, conscience-stricken at having wasted so much of your precious time in reading, and feeling yourself, as you prettily said, 'quite useless to me,' you went to my drawers and hunted out some unhemmed pocket handkerchiefs, and by no means could I prevail upon you to resume your story-books till you had hemmed them all. I remember, too, your teaching my little maid to read, your sitting with her a whole evening to console her for the death of her sister, and that she in her turn endeavored to become a comforter to you the next evening, when you wept at the sight of Mrs. Holcroft, from whose school you had recently eloped because you were not partial to sitting in the stocks. Those tears, and a few you dropped when my brother teased you about your supposed fondness for an apple dumpling, were the only interruptions to the calm contentedness of your unclouded brow.

"We still remain the same as you left us, neither taller nor wiser, or perceptibly older; but three years must have made a great alteration in you. How very much, dear Barbara, I should like to see you!

"We still live in Temple Lane, but I am now sitting in a room you never saw. Soon after you left us we were distressed by the cries of a cat, which seemed to proceed from the garrets adjoining to ours, and only separated from ours by a locked door on the farther side of my brother's bed-room, which you know was the little room at the top of the kitchen stairs. We had the lock forced, and let poor puss out from behind a panel of the wainscot, and she lived with us from that time, for we were in gratitude bound to keep her, as she had introduced us to four untenanted, unowned rooms, and by degrees we have taken possession of these unclaimed apartments, first putting up lines to dry our clothes, then moving my brother's bed into one of these, more commodious than his own rooms; and last winter, my brother being unable to pursue a work he had begun, owing to the kind interruptions of friends who were more at leisure than himself, I persuaded him that he might write at ease in one of these rooms, as he could not then hear the door-knock, or hear himself denied to be at home, which was sure to make him call out and convict the poor maid in a fib. Here, I said, he might be, almost really not at home. So I put in an old grate, and made him a fire in the largest of these garrets, and carried in his own table and one chair, and bid him write away and consider himself as much alone as if he were in a lodging in the midst of Salisbury Plain, or any other wide, unfrequented place where he could expect few visitors to break in upon his solitude. I left him quite delighted with his new acquisition; but in a few hours he came down again, with a sadly dismal face. He could do nothing, he said, with those bare, whitewashed walls before his eyes. He could not write in that dull, unfurnished prison!

"The next day, before he came home from his office, I had gathered up various bits of old carpeting to cover the floor; and to a little break the blank look of the bare walls I hung up a few old prints that used to ornament the kitchen; and after dinner, with great boast of what improvement I had made, I took Charles once more into his new study. A week of busy labors followed, in which I think you would not have disliked to be our assistant. My brother and I almost covered the walls with prints, for which purpose he cut out every print from every book in his old library, coming in every now and then to ask my leave to strip a fresh poor author, which he might not do, you know, without my permission, as I am an elder sister. There was such pasting, such consultation upon these portraits, and where the series of pictures from Ovid, Milton and Shakespeare would show to most advantage, and in what obscure corners authors of humble rank should be allowed to tell their stories. All the books gave up their stores but one, a translation from Ariosto, a delicious set of four-and-twenty prints, and for which I had marked out a conspicuous place; when lo! we found, at the moment the scissors were going to work, that a part of the poem was printed at the back of every picture. What a cruel disappointment! To conclude this long story about nothing, the poor, despised garret is now called the print-room, and is become our most familiar sitting-room. . . . The lions still live in Exeter Change. Returning home through the Strand, I often

hear them roar about twelve o'clock at night.
I never hear them without thinking of you,
because you seemed so pleased with the sight
of them, and said your young companions would
stare when you told them you had seen a lion.

"And now, my dear Barbara, farewell. I
have not written such a long letter a long time,
but I am very sorry I had nothing amusing to
write about. Wishing you may pass happily
through the rest of your school-days and every
future day of your life,

"I remain

"Your affectionate friend,

"M. LAMB.

"My brother sends his love to you. You
say you are not so tall as Louisa — you must
be; you cannot so degenerate from the rest of
your family." ["The measureless Bethams,"
Lamb called them.] "Now you have begun, I
shall hope to have the pleasure of hearing from
you again. I shall always receive a letter from
you with very great delight."

The next is a joint letter to Wordsworth,
in acknowledgment of an early copy of *The
Excursion*, in which Charles holds the pen and
is the chief spokesman; but Mary puts in a
judicious touch of her own : —

"AUGUST 14th, 1814.

"I cannot tell you how pleased I was at the receipt of the great armful of poetry which you have sent me; and to get it before the rest of the world, too! I have gone quite through with it, and was thinking to have accomplished that pleasure a second time before I wrote to thank you, but Mr. Burney came in the night (while we were out) and made holy theft of it; but we expect restitution in a day or two. It is the noblest conversational poem I ever read — a day in Heaven. The part (or rather main body) which has left the sweetest odor on my memory (a bad term for the remains of an impression so recent) is the *Tales of the Church-yard;* the only girl among seven brethren born out of due time, and not duly taken away again; the deaf man and the blind man; the Jacobite and the Hanoverian, whom antipathies recon-cile; the Scarron entry of the rusticating par-son upon his solitude; — these were all new to me too. My having known the story of Mar-garet (at the beginning), a very old acquaint-ance, even as long back as when I first saw you at Stowey, did not make her reappearance less fresh. I don't know what to pick out of this best of books upon the best subjects for partial naming. That gorgeous sunset is famous; I think it must have been the identical one we

saw on Salisbury Plain five years ago, that drew
Phillips from the card-table, where he had sat
from the rise of that luminary to its unequalled
set ; but neither he nor I had gifted eyes to see
those symbols of common things glorified, such
as the prophet saw them in that sunset — the
wheel, the potter's clay, the wash-pot, the wine-
press, the almond-tree rod, the basket of figs,
the four-fold visaged head, the throne and Him
that sat thereon." [It was a mist glorified by
sunshine, not a sunset, which the poet had
described, as Lamb afterwards discovered.]
" One feeling I was particularly struck with, as
what I recognized so very lately at Harrow
Church on entering it after a hot and secular
day's pleasure, the instantaneous coolness, and
calming, almost transforming, properties of a
country church just entered ; a certain fra-
grance which it has, either from its holiness or
being kept shut all the week, or the air that is
let in being pure country, exactly what you
have reduced into words ; but I am feeling that
which I cannot express. Reading your lines
about it fixed me for a time, a monument in
Harrow Church. Do you know it ? With its
fine long spire, white as washed marble, to be
seen, by vantage of its high site, as far as Salisbury spire itself, almost.

" I shall select a day or two very shortly, when

I am coolest in brain, to have a steady second
reading, which I feel will lead to many more, for
it will be a stock-book with me while eyes or
spectacles shall be lent me. There is a great
deal of noble matter about mountain scenery,
yet not so much as to overpower and discounte-
nance a poor Londoner or south countryman
entirely, though Mary seems to have felt it
occasionally a little too powerfully ; for it was
her remark during reading it that by your
system it was doubtful if a liver in towns had a
soul to be saved. She almost trembled for that
invisible part of us in her.

" C. Lamb and Sister."

Manning, who had lately been "tarrying on
the skirts of creation" in far Thibet and Tartary, beyond the reach even of letters, now at
last, in 1815, appeared once more on the horizon
at the "half-way house" of Canton, to which
place Lamb hazarded a letter — a most incomparable "lying letter," and another to confess
the cheat, to St. Helena : — "Have you recovered the breathless, stone-staring astonishment
into which you must have been thrown upon
learning at landing that an Emperor of France
was living in St. Helena ? What an event in
the solitude of the seas ! like finding a fish's
bone at the top of Plinlimmon. . . . Mary

reserves a portion of your silk, not to be buried in (as the false Nuncio asserts), but to make up spick and span into a brand-new gown to wear when you come. I am the same as when you knew me, almost to a surfeiting identity. This very night I am going to *leave off tobacco!* Surely there must be some other world in which this unconquerable purpose shall be realized. The soul hath not her generous aspirings implanted in her in vain."

Manning brought with him on his return much material for compiling a Chinese dictionary; which purpose, however, remained unfulfilled. He left no other memorial of himself than his friendship with Lamb. "You see but his husk or shrine. He discloses not, save to select worshipers, and will leave the world without any one hardly but me knowing how stupendous a creature he is," said Lamb of him. Henceforth their intercourse was chiefly personal.

Coleridge, also, who of late had been almost as much lost to his friends as if he too were in Tartary or Thibet, though now and then "like a reappearing star" standing up before them when least expected, was at the beginning of April, 1816, once more in London, endeavoring to get his tragedy of *Remorse* accepted at Covent Garden. "Nature, who conducts every

creature by instinct to its best end, has skil-
fully directed C. to take up his abode at a chem-
ist's laboratory in Norfolk street," writes Lamb
to Wordsworth.   "She might as well have
sent a *Helluo Librórum* for cure to the Vatican.
He has done pretty well as yet. Tell Miss
Hutchinson my sister is every day wishing to
be quietly sitting down to answer her very kind
letter, but while C. stays she can hardly find a
quiet time.   God bless him !"

But Coleridge was more in earnest than Lamb
supposed in his determination to break through
his thraldom to opium.   Either way, he himself
believed that death was imminent : to go on
was deadly, and a physician of eminence had
told him that to abstain altogether would probably be equally fatal.   He therefore found a
medical man willing to undertake the care of
him ; to exercise absolute surveillance for a
time and watch the results.   It is an affecting
letter in which he commits himself into Mr.
Gillman's hands : "You will never *hear* anything but truth from me. Prior habits render
it out of my power to tell an untruth, but unless
carefully observed I dare not promise that I
should not, with regard to this detested poison,
be capable of acting one. . . . For the first
week I must not be permitted to leave your
house, unless with you. Delicately or indeli-

cately, this must be done, and both the servants
and the assistant must receive absolute com-
mands from you. The stimulus of conversation
suspends the terror that haunts my mind; but
when I am alone the horrors I have suffered
from laudanum, the degradation, the blighted
utility, almost overwhelm me. If (as I feel for
the *first time* a soothing confidence it will
prove) I should leave you restored to my moral
and bodily health, it is not myself only that will
love and honor you; every friend I have (and,
thank God! in spite of this wretched vice I
have many and warm ones, who were friends of
my youth and have never deserted me) will
thank you with reverence." That confidence
was justified, those thanks well earned. In the
middle of April, 1816, Coleridge took up his
abode with the Gilmans at No. 3, the Grove, at
Highgate, and found there a serene haven in
which he anchored for the rest of life; freeing
himself by slow degrees from the opium bond-
age, though too shattered in frame ever to
recover sound health; too far spent, morally
and mentally, by the long struggles and abase-
ments he had gone through to renew the splen-
dors of his youth. That "shaping spirit of
imagination" with which nature had endowed
him drooped languidly, save in fitful moments
of fervid talk; that "fertile, subtle, expansive

understanding " could not fasten with the long-sustained intensity needful to grapple victoriously with the great problems that filled his mind.   The look of "timid earnestness " which Carlyle noted in his eyes expressed a mental attitude — a mixture of boldness and fear, a desire to seek truth at all hazards, yet also to drag authority with him, as a safe and comfortable prop to rest on.   But his eloquence had lost none of its richness and charm, his voice none of its sweetness.   "His face, when he repeats his verses, hath its ancient glory, — an archangel a little damaged," says Lamb to Wordsworth.   "He is absent but four miles, and the neighborhood of such a man is as exciting as the presence of fifty ordinary persons. 'Tis enough to be within the whiff and wind of his genius for us not to possess our souls in quiet."

Besides the renewed proximity of these two oldest and dearest of friends, two new ones, both very young, both future biographers of Lamb, were in these years added to the number of his intimates, — Talfourd in 1815, Proctor in 1817.   Leigh Hunt had become one probably as early as 1812; Crabb Robinson in 1806; Thomas Hood, who stood in the front rank of his younger friends, and Bernard Barton, the Quaker poet, Lamb's chief correspondent dur-

ing the last ten years of his life, not until
1822–3.

The years did not pass without each bringing
a recurrence of one, sometimes of two, severe
attacks of Mary's disorder. In the autumn of
1815 Charles repeats again the sad story to
Miss Hutchinson :—

"I am forced to be the replier to your letter,
for Mary has been ill and gone from home these
five weeks yesterday. She has left me very
lonely and very miserable. I stroll about ; but
there is no rest but at one's own fire-side, and
there is no rest for me there now. I look forward to the worse half being past, and keep up
as well as I can. She has begun to show some
favorable symptoms. The return of her disorder has been frightfully soon this time, with
scarce a six-months' interval. I am almost
afraid my worry of spirits about the E. I. House
was partly the cause of her illness ; but one
always imputes it to the cause next at hand ;
more probably it comes from some cause we
have no control over or conjecture of. It cuts
sad, great slices out of the time, the little time
we shall have to live together. I don't know but
the recurrence of these illnesses might help me
to sustain her death better than if we had no
partial separations. But I won't talk of death.
I will imagine us immortal, or forget that we are

otherwise. By God's blessing, in a few weeks
we may be taking our meal together, or sitting
in the front row of the pit at Drury Lane, or
taking our evening walk past the theaters, to
look at the outside of them at least, if not to be
tempted in. Then we forget we are assailable;
we are strong for the time as rocks — 'the
wind is tempered to the shorn Lambs.' Poor
C. Lloyd" [he was suffering from the same
dread malady]! "poor Priscilla! I feel I hardly
feel enough for him; my own calamities press
about me and involve me in a thick integument
not to be reached at by other folks' misfortunes. But I feel all I can — all the kindness I
can towards you all."

More and more sought by an enlarging circle
of friends, chambers in the Temple offered
facilities for the dropping in of acquaintance
upon the Lambs at all hours of the day and
night, which, social as they were, was harassing,
wearing, and to Mary very injurious. This it
was, doubtless, which induced them to take the
step announced by her in the following letter
to Dorothy Wordsworth :—

"NOVEMBER 21, 1817.

"Your kind letter has given us very much
pleasure; the sight of your handwriting was a
most welcome surprise to us. We have heard

good tidings of you by all our friends who were so fortunate as to visit you this summer, and rejoice to see it confirmed by yourself. You have quite the advantage in volunteering a letter; there is no merit in replying to so welcome a stranger.

"We have left the Temple. I think you will be sorry to hear this. I know I have never been so well satisfied with thinking of you at Rydal Mount as when I could connect the idea of you with your own Grasmere Cottage. Our rooms were dirty and out of repair, and the inconveniences of living in chambers became every year more irksome, and so at last we mustered up resolution enough to leave the good old place that so long had sheltered us, and here we are, living at a brazier's shop, No. 20, in Russell street, Covent Garden, a place all alive with noise and bustle; Drury Lane Theater in sight from our front and Covent Garden from our back windows. The hubbub of the carriages returning from the play does not annoy me in the least; strange that it does not, for it is quite tremendous. I quite enjoy looking out of the window and listening to the calling up of the carriages and the squabbles of the coachmen and link-boys. It is the oddest scene to look down upon; I am sure you would be amused with it. It is well I am in a cheerful place, or I should have many misgivings about leaving the Temple. I look forward with great pleasure to the prospect of seeing my good friend, Miss Hutchinson. I wish Rydal Mount, with all its inhabitants inclosed, were to be transplanted with her, and to remain stationary in the midst of Covent Garden. I passed through the street lately where Mr. and Mrs. Wordsworth lodged; several fine new houses, which were then just rising out of the ground, are quite finished, and a noble entrance made that way into Portland place. I am very sorry for Mr. De Quincey. What a blunder the poor man made when he took up his dwelling among the mountains! I long to see my friend Pypos. Coleridge is still at Little Hampton with Mrs. Gillman; he has been so ill as to be confined to his room almost the whole time he has been there.

"Charles has had all his Hogarths bound in a book; they were sent home yesterday, and now that I have them all together, and perceive the advantage of peeping close at them through my spectacles, I am reconciled to the loss of their hanging round the room, which has been a great mortification to me. In vain I tried to console myself with looking at our new chairs and carpets, for we have got new chairs and carpets covering all over our two sitting-rooms; I missed my old friends and could not be comforted. Then I would resolve to learn to look out of the window, a habit I never could attain in my life, and I have given it up as a thing quite impracticable; yet, when I was at Brighton last summer, the first week I never took my eyes off from the sea, not even to look in a book: I had not seen the sea for sixteen years. Mrs. Morgan, who was with us, kept her liking, and continued her seat in the window till the very last, while Charles and I played truants and wandered among the hills, which we magnified into little mountains, and *almost as good as* Westmoreland scenery. Certainly we made discoveries of many pleasant walks, which few of the Brighton visitors have ever dreamed of; for, like as is the case in the neighborhood of London, after the first two or three miles we are sure to find ourselves in a perfect solitude. I hope we shall meet before the walking faculties of either of us fail. You say you can walk fifteen miles with ease; that is exactly my stint, and more fatigues me; four or five miles every third or fourth day, keeping very quiet between, was all Mrs. Morgan could accomplish. God bless you and yours. Love to all and each one."

In the spring of 1820 the Lambs took lodgings at Stoke Newington, without, however, giving up the Russell street home,— for the sake of rest and quiet; the change from the Temple to Covent Garden not having proved much of a success in that respect, and the need grown serious. Even Lamb's mornings at the office and his walk thence were besieged by officious acquaintance: then, as he tells Wordsworth, "Up I go, mutton on table, hungry as a hunter, hope to forget my cares, and bury them in the agreeable abstraction of mastication. Knock at the door; in comes Mr. Hazlitt, or Mr. Burney, or Morgan Demi-Gorgon, or my brother, or somebody, to prevent my eating alone — a process absolutely necessary to my poor wretched digestion. Oh, the pleasure of eating alone! eating my dinner alone! let me think of it. But in they come, and make it absolutely necessary that I should open a bottle of orange; for my meat turns into a stone when any one dines with me if I have not wine. Wine can mollify stones; then *that* wine turns into acidity, acerbity, misanthropy, a hatred of my interrupters (God bless 'em! I love some of 'em dearly), and with the hatred a still greater aversion to their going away. Bad is the dead sea they bring upon me, choking and deadening; but worse is the deader dry sand they leave me on if they go before bed-time. Come never, I would say to these spoilers of my dinner ; but if you come, never go ! . . . Evening company I should like, had I any mornings, but I am saturated with human faces (*divine*, forsooth !) and voices all the golden morning ; and five evenings in a week would be as much as I should covet to be in company ; but I assure you that is a wonderful week in which I can get two or one to myself. I am never C. L., but always C. L. & Co. He who thought it not good for man to be alone preserve me from the more prodigious monstrosity of being never by myself ! I forget bed-time, but even there these sociable frogs clamber up to annoy me." . . .

It was during the Russell street days that the Lambs made the acquaintance of Vincent Novello. He had a little daughter, Mary Victoria, afterwards Mrs. Cowden Clarke, whose heart Mary won, leaving many sweet and happy impressions of herself graven there, which eventually took shape in her *Recollections of Writers*. Mrs. Novello had lost a baby in the spring of 1820, and from the quiet of Stoke Newington Mary wrote her a sweet letter of condolence :—

"Spring, 1820.

"Since we heard of your sad sorrow, you have been perpetually in our thoughts ; therefore you may well imagine how welcome your

kind remembrance of us must be. I know
not how to thank you for it. You bid me
write a long letter; but my mind is so possessed
with the idea that you must be occupied with
one only thought, that all trivial matters seem
impertinent. I have just been reading again
Mr. Hunt's delicious essay [*Deaths of Little
Children*], which, I am sure, must have come
so home to your hearts. I shall always love
him for it. I feel that it is all that one can
think, but which no one but he could have done
so prettily. May he lose the memory of his
own babies in seeing them all grow old around
him. Together with the recollection of your
dear baby, the image of a little sister I once
had comes as fresh into my mind as if I had
seen her lately. . . . I long to see you, and I
hope to do so on Tuesday or Wednesday in
next week. Percy street! I love to write the
word. What comfortable ideas it brings with
it! We have been pleasing ourselves, ever
since we heard this unexpected piece of good
news, with the anticipation of frequent drop-in
visits and all the social comfort of what seems
almost next-door neighborhood.

"Our solitary confinement has answered its
purpose even better than I expected. It is so
many years since I have been out of town in
the spring that I scarcely knew of the existence

of such a season. I see every day some new
flower peeping out of the ground, and watch its
growth ; so that I have a sort of intimate friendship with each. I know the effect of every
change of weather upon them — have learned
all their names, the duration of their lives, and
the whole progress of their domestic economy.
My landlady, a nice, active old soul that wants
but one year of eighty, and her daughter, a
rather aged young gentlewoman, are the only
laborers in a pretty large garden ; for it is a
double house, and two long strips of ground are
laid into one, well stored with fruit-trees, which
will be in full blossom the week after I am
gone, and flowers, as many as can be crammed
in, of all sorts and kinds. But flowers are
flowers still ; and I must confess I would rather
live in Russell street all my life, and never set
my foot but on London pavement, than be
doomed always to enjoy the silent pleasures I
now do. We go to bed at ten o'clock. Late
hours are life-shortening things, but I would
rather run all risks, and sit every night — at
some places I could name — wishing in vain at
eleven o'clock for the entrance of the supper
tray, than be always up and alive at eight
o'clock breakfast, as I am here. We have a
scheme to reconcile these things. We have an
offer of a very low-rented lodging a mile nearer

town than this. Our notion is to divide our time in alternate weeks between quiet rest and dear London weariness. We give an answer to-morrow; but what that will be at this present writing I am unable to say. In the present state of our undecided opinion, a very heavy rain that is now falling may turn the scale. . . . Dear rain, do go away, and let us have a fine, chearful sunset to argue the matter fairly in. My brother walked seventeen miles yesterday before dinner. And, notwithstanding his long walk to and from the office, we walk every evening; but I by no means perform in this way so well as I used to do. A twelve-mile walk, one hot Sunday morning, made my feet blister, and they are hardly well now." . . .

"A fine, cheerful sunset" did smile, it seems, upon the project of permanent country lodgings; for during the next three years the Lambs continued to alternate between "dear London weariness" in Russell street, and rest and quiet work at Dalston. Years they were which produced nearly all the most delightful of the *Essays of Elia.*

The year 1821 closed gloomily: "I stepped into the Lambs' cottage at Dalston," writes Crabb Robinson in his diary, Nov. 18. "Mary pale and thin, just recovered from one of her attacks. They have lost their brother John and feel the loss." And the very same week died fine old Captain Burney. He had been made Admiral but a fortnight before his death. These gaps among the old familiar faces struck chill to their hearts. In a letter to Wordsworth, of the following spring, Lamb says: "We are pretty well, save colds and rheumatics, and a certain deadness to everything, which I think I may date from poor John's loss, and another accident or two at the same time that have made me almost bury myself at Dalston, where yet I see more faces than I could wish. Deaths overset one and put one out long after the recent grief. Two or three have died within the last two twelvemonths, and so many parts of me have been numbed. One sees a picture, reads an anecdote, starts a casual fancy, and thinks to tell of it to this person in preference to every other; the person is gone whom it would have peculiarly suited. It won't do for another. Every departure destroys a class of sympathies. There's Captain Burney gone! What fun has whist now? What matters it what you lead if you can no longer fancy him looking over you? One never hears anything, but the image of the particular person occurs with whom alone, almost, you would care to share the intelligence. Thus one distributes one's self about, and now for so many parts of

me I have lost the market." It was while
John's death was yet recent that Lamb wrote
some tender recollections of him (fact and
fiction blended according to "Elia's" wont) in
Dream Children, a Reverie, telling how handsome and spirited he had been in his youth,
"and how, when he died, though he had not
been dead an hour, it seemed as if he had died
a great while ago, such a distance there is
betwixt life and death; and how I bore his
death, as I thought, pretty well at first, but
afterwards it haunted and haunted me; and
though I did not cry or take it to heart as some
do, and as I think he would have done if I had
died, yet I missed him all day long, and knew
not till then how much I had loved him. I
missed his kindness and I missed his crossness,
and wished him to be alive again to be quarreling with him (for we quarreled sometimes),
rather than not have him again."

CHAPTER XIV.

1822-3. — Æt. 58-59.

FOR some years matters had not gone smoothly
between Sara Hazlitt and her husband. He
was hard to live with, and she seems to have
given up the attempt to make the best of things,
and to have sunk into a kind of apathy in which
even the duties of a housewife were ill performed ; but his chief complaint was that "she
despised him and his abilities." In this, Hazlitt was, probably, unjust to Sara ; for she was
neither stupid nor unamiable. From 1819
onwards he had absented himself from home
continually, living either at the Huts, a small
inn on the edge of Salisbury Plain, or in London lodgings. But in this year of 1822 his
unhappy passion for Sarah Walker brought
about a crisis ; and what had been only a neg-
ative kind of evil became unendurable. He
prevailed upon Sara to consent to a divorce.

It was obtained, in Edinburgh, by Mrs. Hazlitt taking what, in Scotch law, is called "the oath of calumny," which — the suit being unde-fended — entitled her to a dissolution of the marriage tie. They then returned singly to Winterslow, he to the Huts and she to her cot-tage. If they married with but little love, they seem to have parted without any hate. One tie remained — the strong affection each had for their son, who was sometimes with one, sometimes with the other. Hazlitt's wholly unrequited passion for Sarah Walker soon burned itself to ashes; and in two years' time he tried another experiment in marriage which was even less successful than the first; for his bride, like Milton's, declined to return home with him after the wedding tour, and he saw her face no more. But, unlike Milton, he was little discomposed at the circumstance. Sara, grown a wiser if not a more dignified woman, did not renew the scheming ways of her youth. She continued to stand high in the esteem of Hazlitt's mother and sister, and often stayed with them. The Lambs abated none of their old cordiality; Mary wrote few letters now, but Charles sent her a friendly one sometimes. It was to her he gave the first account of absent-minded George Dyer's feat of walking straight into the New River, in broad daylight, on leav-

ing their door in Colebrook Row. Towards
Hazlitt, also, their friendship seemed substan-
tially unchanged, let him be as splenetic and
wayward as he might. "We cannot afford to
cast off our friends because they are not all we
could wish," said Mary Lamb once when he had
written some criticisms on Wordsworth and
Coleridge, in which glowing admiration was
mixed with savage ridicule in such a way that,
as Lamb said, it was "like saluting a man:
'Sir, you are the greatest man I ever saw,' and
then pulling him by the nose." But it needed
only for Hazlitt himself to be traduced and vil-
ified, as he so often was, by the political adver-
saries and critics of those days, for Lamb to
rally to his side and fearlessly pronounce him
to be, "in his natural and healthy state, one of
the wisest and finest spirits breathing."

As a set-off against the already mentioned
sorrows of this time, a new element of cheerfulness was introduced into the Lamb household; for it was in the course of the summer
of 1823 that, during a visit to Cambridge, they
first saw Emma Isola, a little orphan child, of
whom they soon grew so fond that eventually
she became their adopted daughter, their solace
and comfort. To Mary especially was this a
happy incident. "For," says Mrs. Cowden-
Clarke in the *Recollections* already alluded to,

"she had a most tender sympathy with the young,"—as the readers of *Mrs. Leicester's School* will hardly need telling. "She was encouraging and affectionate towards them, and won them to regard her with a familiarity and fondness rarely felt by them for grown people who are not their relations. She threw herself so entirely into their way of thinking and contrived to take an estimate of things so completely from *their* point of view, that she made them rejoice to have her for their co-mate in affairs that interested them. While thus lending herself to their notions, she, with a judiciousness peculiar to her, imbued her words with the wisdom and experience that belonged to her maturer years; so that while she seemed but the listening, concurring friend, she was also the helping, guiding friend. Her monitions never took the form of reproof, but were always dropped in with the air of agreed propositions, as if they grew out of the subject in question, and presented themselves as matters of course to both her young companions and herself." The following is a life-like picture, from the same hand, of Mary among the children she gathered round her in these Russell street days — Hazlitt's little son William, Victoria Novello (Mrs. Clarke herself) and Emma Isola. Victoria used "to come to

her on certain mornings, when Miss Lamb
promised to hear her repeat her Latin grammar,
and hear her read poetry with the due music-
ally rhythmical intonation. Even now the
breathing murmur of the voice in which Mary
Lamb gave low but melodious utterance to
those opening lines of the *Paradise Lost:*—

> Of man's first disobedience, and the fruit
> Of that forbidden tree, whose mortal taste
> Brought death into the world and all our woe,—

sounding full and rounded and harmonious,
though so subdued in tone, rings clear and
distinct in the memory of her who heard the
reader. The echo of that gentle voice vibrates,
through the lapse of many a revolving year,
true and unbroken in the heart where the low,
breathed sound first awoke response, teaching
together with the fine appreciation of verse-
music the finer love of intellect conjoined with
goodness and kindness. . . . One morning,
just as Victoria was about to repeat her allotted
task, in rushed a young boy who, like herself,
enjoyed the privilege of Miss Lamb's instruction in the Latin language. His mode of
entrance, hasty and abrupt, sufficiently denoted
his eagerness to have his lesson heard at once
and done with, that he might be gone again;
accordingly Miss Lamb, asking Victoria to give

10

up her turn, desired the youth, Hazlitt's son, to repeat his pages of grammar first. Off he set; rattled through the first conjugation post-haste; darted through the second without drawing breath; and so on right through in no time. The rapidity, the volubility, the triumphant slap-dash of the feat perfectly dazzled the imagination of poor Victoria, who stood admiring by, an amazed witness of the boy's proficiency. She herself, a quiet, plodding little girl, had only by dint of diligent study and patient, persevering poring, been able to achieve a slow learning and as slow a repetition of her lessons. This brilliant, off-hand method of dispatching the Latin grammar was a glory she had never dreamed of. Her ambition was fired, and the next time she presented herself book in hand before Miss Lamb, she had no sooner delivered it into her hearer's than she attempted to scour through her verb at the same rattling pace which had so excited her admiration. Scarce a moment and her stumbling scamper was checked. 'Stay, stay! how's this? What are you about, little Vicky?' asked the laughing voice of Mary Lamb. 'Oh, I see. Well, go on; but gently, gently; no need of hurry.' She heard to an end, and then said: 'I see what we have been doing — trying to be as quick and clever as William, fancying

it vastly grand to get on at a great rate, as he does. But there's this difference : it's natural in him, while it's imitation in you. Now, far better go on in your old staid way—which is your own way — than try to take up a way that may become him, but can never become you, even were you to succeed in acquiring it. We'll each of us keep to our own natural ways, and then we shall be sure to do our best.' And when Victoria and Emma Isola met there, Mary entered into their girlish friendship; let them have their gossip out in her own room if tired of the restraint of grown-up company; and once, before Emma's return to school, took them to Dulwich and gave them a charming little dinner of roast fowl and custard pudding."
. . . "Pleasant above all," says the surviving guest and narrator, "is the memory of the cordial voice, which said, in a way to put the little party at its fullest ease, 'Now, remember, we all pick our bones. It isn't considered vulgar here to pick bones.'

"Once, when some visitors chanced to drop in unexpectedly upon her and her brother," continues Mrs. Clarke, "just as they were sitting down to their plain dinner of a bit of roast mutton, with her usual frank hospitality she pressed them to stay and partake, cutting up the small joint into five equal portions, and say-

ing in her simple, easy way, so truly her own :
'There's a chop apiece for us, and we can make
up with bread and cheese if we want more.'"

The more serious demands upon her sympathy and judgment made, after childhood was
left behind, by the young, whether man or
woman, she met with no less tenderness, tact
and wisdom. Once, for instance, when she
thought she perceived symptoms of an unex-
plained dejection in her young friend Victoria,
"how gentle was her sedate mode of reasoning
the matter, after delicately touching upon the
subject and endeavoring to draw forth its
avowal! More as if mutually discussing and consulting than as if questioning, she endeavored
to ascertain whether uncertainties or scruples
of faith had arisen in the young girl's mind and
had caused her preoccupied, abstracted manner.
If it were any such source of disturbance, how
wisely and feelingly she suggested reading,
reflecting, weighing ; if but a less deeply-seated
depression, how sensibly she advised adopting
some object to rouse energy and interest ! She
pointed out the efficacy of studying a language
(she herself at upwards of fifty years of age
began the acquirement of French and Italian)
as a remedial measure, and advised Victoria to
devote herself to a younger brother she had,
in the same way that she had attended to her

own brother Charles in his infancy, as the wholesomest and surest means of all for cure."

Allsop, Coleridge's friend, speaks in the same strain of how when a young man, overwhelmed with what then seemed the hopeless ruin of his prospects, he found Charles and Mary Lamb not wanting in the hour of need. "I have a clear recollection," says he, "of Miss Lamb's addressing me in a tone which acted at once as a solace and support, and after as a stimulus, to which I owe more perhaps than to the more extended arguments of all others."

On the whole Mary was a silent woman. It was her forte rather to enable others to talk their best by the charm of an earnest, speaking countenance and a responsive manner; and there are but few instances in which any of her words have been preserved. In that memorable conversation at Lamb's table on "persons one would like to have seen," reported by Hazlitt, when it was a question of women: "I should like vastly to have seen Ninon de L'Enclos," said Mary. When Queen Caroline's trial was pending and her character and conduct the topic in every mouth, Mary said she did not see that it made much difference whether the Queen was what they called guilty or not — meaning, probably, that the stream was so plainly muddy at the fountain-head, it was idle to inquire what ill places it had passed through in its course. Or else, perhaps, that, either way, the King's conduct was equally odious.

The last observation of hers I can find recorded is at first sight unlike herself: "How stupid old people are!" It was that unimaginative incapacity to sympathize with the young, so alien to her own nature, no doubt, which provoked the remark. Of her readiness to help all that came within her reach there is a side-glimpse in some letters of Lamb's — the latest to see the light, — which come, as other interesting contributions to the knowledge of Lamb's writings have done (notably those of the late Mr. Babson), from over the Atlantic. In *The Century* magazine for September, 1882, are seven letters to John Howard Payne, an American playwright, whom Lamb was endeavoring to help in his but partially successful struggle to earn a livelihood by means of adaptations for the stage in London and Paris. Mrs. Cowden Clarke speaks of this Mr. Payne as the acquaintance whom Mary Lamb, "ever thoughtful to procure a pleasure for young people," had asked to call and see the little Victoria, then at school at Boulogne, on his way to Paris. He proved a good friend to Mary herself during that trip to France which, with a courage amounting to rashness, she and Charles undertook in the summer of 1822.

" I went to call on the Lambs to take leave,
they setting out for France next morning,"
writes Crabb Robinson in his diary, June 17th.
" I gave Miss Lamb a letter for Miss Williams,
to whom I sent a copy of *Mrs. Leicester's School.*
The Lambs have a Frenchman as their companion, and Miss Lamb's nurse, in case she should
be ill. Lamb was in high spirits; his sister
rather nervous."

The privation of sleep entailed in such a journey, combined with the excitement, produced
its inevitable result, and Mary was taken with
one of her severest attacks in the diligence on
the way to Amiens. There, happily, they seem
to have found Mr. Payne, who assisted Charles
to make the necessary arrangements for her
remaining under proper care till the return of
reason, and then he went on to Paris, where he
stayed with the Kennys, who thought him dull
and out of sorts, as well he might be. Two
months afterwards we hear of Mary as being
in Paris. Charles, his holiday over, had been
obliged to return to England.

" Mary Lamb has begged me to give her a
day or two," says Crabb Robinson. " She
comes to Paris this evening and stays here a
week. Her only male friend is a Mr. Payne,
whom she praises exceedingly for his kindness
and attentions to Charles. He is the author of
Brutus, and has a good face."

It was in the following year that most of the letters to Mr. Payne, published in the *Century*, were written. They disclose Mary and her brother zealous to repay one good turn with another by watching the success of his dramatic efforts and endeavoring to negotiate favorably for him with actors and managers: "*Ali Pacha* will do. I sent my sister the first night, not having been able to go myself, and her report of its effect was most favorable. . . . My love to my little wife at Versailles, and to her dear mother. . . . I have no mornings (my day begins at 5 P. M.) to transact business in, or talents for it, so I employ Mary, who has seen Robertson, who says that the piece which is to be operafied was sent to you six weeks since, etc., etc. Mary says you must write more *showable* letters about these matters, for with all our trouble of crossing out this word, and giving a cleaner turn to th' other, and folding down at this part, and squeezing an obnoxious epithet into a corner, she can hardly communicate their contents without offense. What, man, put less gall in your ink, or write me a biting tragedy!" . . .

The piece which was sent to Mr. Payne in Paris to be "operafied" was probably *Clari, the Maid of Milan*. Bishop wrote or adapted the music: it still keeps possession of the stage, and contains "Home, Sweet Home," which plaintive, well-worn ditty earned for its writer among his friends the title of the "Homeless Poet of Home." He ended his days as American Consul at Tunis.

This year's holiday (1823), spent at Hastings, was one of unalloyed pleasure and refreshment. "I have given up my soul to walking," Lamb writes. "There are spots, inland bays, etc., which realize the notions of Juan Fernandez. The best thing I lit upon, by accident, was a small country church (by whom or when built unknown), standing bare and single in the midst of a grove, with no house or appearance of habitation within a quarter of a mile, only passages diverging from it through beautiful woods to so many farm-houses. There it stands, like the first idea of a church, before parishioners were thought of, nothing but birds for its congregation; or like a hermit's oratory (the hermit dead), or a mausoleum; its effect singularly impressive, like a church found in a desert isle to startle Crusoe with a home image. . . . I am a long time reconciling to town after one of these excursions. Home is become strange, and will remain so yet awhile; home is the most unforgiving of friends, and always resents absence; I know its cordial looks will return, but they are slow in clearing up."

The "cordial looks," however, of the Russell
street home never did return.   The plan of the
double lodgings, there and at Dalston, was a
device of double discomforts ; the more so as
"at my town lodgings," he afterwards confesses
to Bernard Barton, "the mistress was always
quarreling with our maid ; and at my place of
rustication the whole family were always beating
one another, brothers beating sisters (one, a
most beautiful girl, lamed for life), father beating sons and daughters, and son again beating
his father, knocking him fairly down, — a scene
I never before witnessed, but was called out of
bed by the unnatural blows, the parricidal color
of which, though my morals could not but con-
demn, yet my reason did heartily approve ; and
in the issue the house was quieter for a day or
so than I had ever known."   It was time,
indeed, for brother and sister to have a house
of their own over their heads, means now amply
sufficing.

A few weeks after their return Lamb took
Colebrook Cottage at Islington.   It was
detached, faced the New River, had six good
rooms, and a spacious garden behind.   "You
enter without passage," he writes, "into a
cheerful dining-room, all studded over and
rough with old books, and above is a lightsome
drawing-room, full of choice prints.   I feel like

a great lord, never having had a house before."

A new acquaintance, a man much after Lamb's heart, at whose table he and Mary were, in the closing years of his life, more frequent guests than at any other — "Mr. Carey, the Dante man," — was added to their list this year. "He is a model of a country parson, — lean (as a curate ought to be), modest, sensible, no obtruder of church dogmas, quite a different man from Southey," says Lamb of him. "Quite a different man from Southey" had a peculiar sting in it at this moment, for Southey had just struck a blow at "Elia" in the *Quarterly*, as unjust in purport as it was odious in manner — detraction in the guise of praise. Lamb answered him this very autumn in the *London Magazine;* a noble answer it is, which seems to have awakened something like compunction in Southey's exemplary but pharisaic soul. At all events he made overtures for a reconciliation, which so touched Lamb's generous heart, he was instantly ready to take blame upon himself for having written the letter. "I shall be ashamed to see you, and my sister, though innocent, still more so," he says, "for the folly was done without her knowledge, and has made her uneasy ever since. My guardian angel was absent at that time." By which token we know that Mary did not escape the usual sad effects of change and fatigue in the removal to Colebrook Cottage.

Means were easy, home comfortable now; but many a wistful, backward glance did brother and sister cast to the days of early struggle, with their fuller life, keener pleasures and better health. It was not long after they were settled in Colebrook Cottage that they opened their hearts on this theme in that beautiful essay by "Elia" called *Old China*, Wordsworth's favorite, in which Charles for once made himself Mary's—or, as he calls her, Cousin Bridget's—mouthpiece. Whilst sipping tea out of "a set of extraordinary blue china, a recent purchase," . . . writes "Elia," " I could not help remarking how favorable circumstances had been to us of late years, that we could afford to please the eye sometimes with trifles of this sort; when a passing sentiment seemed to overshade the brow of my companion. I am quick at detecting these summer clouds in Bridget.

"'I wish the good old times would come again,' she said, 'when we were not quite so rich. I do not mean that I want to be poor; but there was a middle state,' so she was pleased to ramble on, 'in which I am sure we were a great deal happier. A purchase is but a purchase, now that you have money enough and to spare. Formerly it used to be a triumph. When we coveted a cheap luxury (and oh, how much ado I had to get you to consent in those times!) we were used to have a debate two or three days before, and to weigh the *for* and *against*, and think what we might spare it out of, and what saving we could hit upon that should be an equivalent. A thing was worth buying then, when we felt the money that we paid for it.

"'Do you remember the brown suit which you made to hang upon you till all your friends cried "Shame upon you!" it grew so thread-bare, and all because of that folio Beaumont and Fletcher, which you dragged home late at night from Barker's in Covent Garden? Do you remember how we eyed it for weeks before we could make up our minds to the purchase, and had not come to a determination till it was near ten o'clock of the Saturday night when you set off from Islington, fearing you should be too late, and when the old bookseller with some grumbling opened his shop, and by the twink-ling taper (for he was setting bedwards) lighted out the relic from his dusty treasures, and when you lugged it home, wishing it were twice as cumbersome, and when you presented it to me, and when we were exploring the perfectness of it (*collating*, you called it), and while I was repairing some of the loose leaves with paste, which your impatience would not suffer to be left till daybreak,—was there no pleasure in being a poor man? Or can those neat black clothes which you wear now, and are so careful to keep brushed since we have become rich and finical, give you half the honest vanity with which you flaunted it about in that over-worn suit, your old corbeau, for four or five weeks longer than you should have done, to pacify your conscience for the mighty sum of fifteen, or sixteen shillings, was it?—a great affair we thought it then—which you had lavished on the old folio? Now you can afford to buy any book that pleases you; but I do not see that you ever bring me home any nice old purchases now.

"'When you came home with twenty apologies for laying out a less number of shillings upon that print after Lionardo which we christened the "Lady Blanch," when you looked at the purchase and thought of the money, and thought of the money and looked again at the picture,—was there no pleasure in being a poor man? Now you have nothing to do but to walk into Colnaghi's and buy a wilderness of Lionardos. Yet, do you?

"'Then do you remember our pleasant walks to Enfield and Potter's Bar and Waltham when

we had a holiday — holidays and all other fun
are gone now we are rich — and the little hand-
basket in which I used to deposit our day's fare
of savory cold lamb and salad, and how you
would pry about at noon-tide for some decent
house where we might go in and produce our
store, only paying for the ale that you must call
for, and speculated upon the looks of the landlady, and whether she was likely to allow us a
table-cloth, and wish for such another honest
hostess as Izaak Walton has described many a
one on the pleasant banks of the Lea when he
went a-fishing? And sometimes they would
prove obliging enough, and sometimes they
would look grudgingly upon us; but we had
cheerful looks still for one another, and would
eat our plain food savorily, scarcely grudging
Piscator his Trout Hall. Now when we go out
a day's pleasuring, which is seldom, moreover,
we *ride* part of the way, and go into a fine inn
and order the best of dinners, never debating
the expense, which after all never has half the
relish of those chance country snaps, when we
were at the mercy of uncertain usage and a
precarious welcome.

"'You are too proud to see a play anywhere
now but in the pit. Do you remember where
it was we used to sit when we saw the " Battle
of Hexham," and the " Surrender of Calais,"

and Bannister and Mrs. Bland in the "Children in the Wood,"— when we squeezed out our shillings apiece to sit three or four times in a season in the one-shilling gallery, where you felt all the time that you ought not to have brought me, and more strongly I felt obligation to you for having brought me — and the pleasure was the better for a little shame? And when the curtain drew up what cared we for our place in the house, or what mattered it where we were sitting, when our thoughts were with Rosalind in Arden or with Viola at the Court of Illyria? You used to say that the gallery was the best place of all for enjoying a play socially; that the relish of such exhibitions must be in proportion to the infrequency of going; that the company we met there, not being in general readers of plays, were obliged to attend the more, and did attend, to what was going on on the stage, because a word lost would have been a chasm which it was impossible for them to fill up. With such reflections we consoled our pride then; and I appeal to you whether as a woman I met generally with less attention and accommodation than I have done since in more expensive situations in the house. The getting in, indeed, and the crowding up those inconvenient staircases, was bad enough, but there was still a law of civility to woman, recognized to quite as great an extent as we ever found in the other passages. And how a little difficulty overcome heightened the snug seat and the play afterwards! Now we can only pay our money and walk in. You cannot see, you say, in the galleries now. I am sure we saw, and heard too, well enough then, but sight and all, I think, is gone with our poverty.

"'There was pleasure in eating strawberries before they became quite common — in the first dish of peas while they were yet dear; to have them for a nice supper, a treat. What treat can we have now? If we were to treat ourselves now — that is, to have dainties a little above our means — it would be selfish and wicked. It is the very little more that we allow ourselves beyond what the actual poor can get at, that makes what I call a treat — when two people, living together as we have done, now and then indulge themselves in a cheap luxury which both like, while each apologizes and is willing to take both halves of the blame to his single share. I see no harm in people making much of themselves in that sense of the word. It may give them a hint how to make much of others. But now — what I mean by the word — we never do make much of ourselves. None but the poor can do it. I do not mean the veriest poor of all, but persons, as we were, just above poverty.

" ' I know what you were going to say — that
it is mighty pleasant at the end of the year to
make all meet, and much ado we used to have
every thirty-first night of December to account
for our exceedings ; many a long face did you
make over your puzzled accounts, and in con-
triving to make it out how we had spent so
much, or that we had not spent so much, or that
it was impossible we should spend so much next
year — and still we found our slender capital
decreasing ; but then, betwixt ways and pro-
jects and compromises of one sort or another,
and talk of curtailing this charge and doing
without that for the future, and the hope that
youth brings and laughing spirits (in which you
were never poor till now), we pocketed up our
loss, and in conclusion, with "lusty brimmers"
(as you used to quote it out of *hearty, cheerful
Mr. Cotton*, as you called him), we used to "welcome in the coming guest." Now we have no
reckonings at all at the end of the old year —
no flattering promises about the new year doing
better for us.'

"Bridget is so sparing of her speech on most
occasions, that when she gets into a rhetorical
vein I am careful how I interrupt it. I could
not help, however, smiling at the phantom of
wealth which her dear imagination had conjured up out of a clear income of poor — hun-

dred pounds a year. It is true we were happier when we were poorer, but we were also younger, my cousin. I am afraid we must put up with the excess, for if we were to shake the superflux into the sea, we should not much mend ourselves. That we had much to struggle with as we grew up together, we have reason to be most thankful. It strengthened and knit our compact closer. We could never have been what we have been to each other, if we had always had the sufficiency which you now complain of. The resisting power, those natural dilations of the youthful spirit, which circumstances cannot straighten, with us are long since passed away. Competence to age is supplementary youth; a sorry supplement indeed, but I fear the best that is to be had. We must ride where we formerly walked; live better and lie softer — and we shall be wise to do so — than we had means to do in those good old days you speak of. Yet could those days return, could you and I once more walk our thirty miles a day, could Bannister and Mrs. Bland again be young, and you and I be young again to see them, — could the good old one-shilling gallery days return — they are dreams, my cousin, now, — but could you and I at this moment, instead of this quiet argument, by our well-carpeted fire-side, sitting on this luxurious sofa, be once more struggling up those inconvenient staircases, pushed about and squeezed and elbowed by the poorest rabble of poor gallery scramblers, — could I once more hear those anxious shrieks of yours, and the delicious ' *Thank God we are safe,*' which always followed when the topmost stair conquered let in the first light of the whole cheerful theater down beneath us, — I know not the fathom-line that ever touched a descent so deep as I would be willing to bury more wealth in than Crœsus had, or the great Jew R. is supposed to have, to purchase it." . . .

These fire-side confidences between brother and sister bring back, in all the warmth and fullness of life, that past mid which the biographer has been groping and listening to echoes.

CHAPTER XV.

Lamb's ill Health. — Retirement from the India House, and subsequent Illness. — Letter from Mary to Lady Stoddart. — Colebrook Cottage left. — Mary's constant Attacks. — Home given up. — Board with the Westwoods. — Death of Hazlitt. — Removal to Edmonton. — Marriage of Emma Isola. — Mary's sudden Recovery. — Ill again. — Death of Coleridge. — Death of Charles. — Mary's last Days and Death.

1824–47. — Æt. 60–83.

THE year 1824 was one of the best Mary ever enjoyed. Alas! it was not the precursor of others like it, but rather a farewell gleam before the clouds gathered up thicker and thicker, till the light of reason was permanently obscured. In November Charles wrote to Miss Hutchinson: "We had promised our dear friends the Monkhouses" [relatives of Mrs. Wordsworth] — "promised ourselves, rather — a visit to them at Ramsgate; but I thought it best, and Mary seemed to have it at heart too, not to go far from home these last holidays. It is connected with a sense of unsettlement, and secretly I know she hoped that such abstinence

would be friendly to her health.   She certainly
has escaped her sad yearly visitation, whether
in consequence of it, or of faith in it, and we
have to be thankful for a good 1824.   To get
such a notion in our heads may go a great way
another year.   Not that we quite confined ourselves ; but, assuming Islington to be head-
quarters, we made timid flights to Ware,
Watford, etc., to try how trouts tasted, for a
night out or so, not long enough to make the
sense of change oppressive, but sufficient to
scour the rust of home."

With Lamb it was quite otherwise.   The
letters of this year show that health and spirits
were flagging sorely.   He had, ever since 1820,
been working at high pressure, producing, in
steady, rapid succession, his matchless essays
in the *London Magazine*, and this at the end
of a long day's office-work.   His delicate,
nervous organization could not fail to suffer
from the continued strain, not to mention the
ever-present and more terrible one of his
sister's health.

At last his looks attracted the notice of one
of his chiefs, and it was intimated that a
resignation might be accepted, as it was after
some anxious delays ; and a provision for Mary,
if she survived, was guaranteed in addition to
his comfortable pension.   The sense of free-

dom was almost overwhelming. "Mary wakes
every morning with an obscure feeling that some
good has happened to us," he writes. "Leigh
Hunt and Montgomery, after their release-
ments, describe the shock of their emancipation
much as I feel mine. But it hurt their frames.
I eat, drink, and sleep as sound as ever."

A reaction did come, however. Lamb continued pretty well through the spring, but in
the summer he was prostrated by a severe
attack of nervous fever. In July he wrote to
Bernard Barton: "My nervous attack has so
unfitted me that I have not courage to sit down
to a letter. My poor pittance in the *London*,
you will see, is drawn from my sickness." [*The
Convalescent*, which appeared July, 1825.]

One more glimpse of Mary in a letter from
her own hand. Again the whole summer was
being spent in lodgings at Enfield, whence Mary
wrote to congratulate her old friend Mrs. (now
Lady) Stoddart, her husband having become
Chief Justice of Malta, on the marriage of a
daughter:—

"AUGUST 9, 1827.

"MY DEAR LADY FRIEND:— My brother
called at our empty cottage [Colebrook] yesterday and found the cards of your son and his
friend, Mr. Hine, under the door, which has
brought to my mind that I am in danger of los-

ing this post, as I did the last, being at that
time in a confused state of mind, — for at that
time we were talking of leaving, and persuading
ourselves that we were intending to leave town
and all our friends, and sit down forever, solitary
and forgotten here. . . . .   Here we are, and
we have locked up our house and left it to take
care of itself; but at present we do not design
to extend our rural life beyond Michaelmas.
Your kind letter was most welcome to me,
though the good news contained in it was
already known to me.   Accept my warmest
congratulations, though they come a little of
the latest.   In my next I may probably have to
hail you grandmamma, or to felicitate you on
the nuptials of pretty Mary, who, whatever the
beaux of Malta may think of her, I can only
remember her round, shining face, and her 'O
William! dear William!' when we visited her
the other day at school.   Present my love and
best wishes, a long and happy married life, to
dear Isabella — I love to call her Isabella; but
in truth, having left your other letter in town,
I recollect no other name she has.   The same
love and the same wishes, *in futuro*, to my
friend Mary.   Tell her that her 'dear William'
grows taller, and improves in manly looks and
man-like behaviour every time I see him.
What is Henry about? and what should one

wish for him? If he be in search of a wife, I will send him out Emma Isola.

"You remember Emma, that you were so kind as to invite to your ball? She is now with us, and I am moving Heaven and earth, that is to say, I am pressing the matter upon all the very few friends I have that are likely to assist me in such a case, to get her into a family as governess; and Charles and I do little else here than teach her something or other all day long.

"We are striving to put enough Latin into her to enable her to begin to teach it to young learners. So much for Emma, for you are so fearfully far away that I fear it is useless to implore your patronage for her. . . .

"I expect a pacquet of manuscript from you. You promised me the office of negotiating with booksellers and so forth for your next work." [Lady Stoddart published several tales under the name of Blackford.] "Is it in good forwardness? Or do you grow rich and indolent now? It is not surprising that your Maltese story should find its way into Malta; but I was highly pleased with the idea of your pleasant surprise at the sight of it. I took a large sheet of paper, in order to leave Charles room to add something more worth reading than my poor mite. May we all meet again once more."

It was to escape the "dear weariness" of incessant friendly visitors, which they were now less than ever able to bear, that they had taken refuge in the Enfield lodging.

"We have been here near three months, and shall stay two more if people will let us alone; but they persecute us from village to village," Lamb writes to Bernard Barton in August.

At the end of that time they decided to return to Colebrook Cottage no more, but to take a house at Enfield. The actual process of taking it was witnessed by a spectator, a perfect stranger at the time, on whose memory it left a lively picture: "Leaning idly out of a window, I saw a group of three issuing from the 'gambogy-looking' cottage close at hand, — a slim, middle-aged man, in quaint, uncontemporary habiliments, a rather shapeless bundle of an old lady, in a bonnet like a mob-cap, and a young girl; while before them bounded a riotous dog (Hood's immortal 'Dash'), holding a board with 'This House to Let' on it in his jaws. Lamb was on his way back to the house-agent, and that was his fashion of announcing that he had taken the premises.

"I soon grew to be on intimate terms with my neighbors," continues the writer of this pleasant reminiscence — Mr. Westwood, in *Notes and Queries*, volume 10 — "who let me loose in his library. . . . My heart yearns even now to those old books. Their faces seem all familiar to me, even their patches and blotches — the work of a wizened old cobbler hard by; for little wotted Lamb of Roger Parkes and Charles Lewises. A cobbler was his bookbinder, and the rougher the restoration the better. . . . When any notable visitors made their appearance at the cottage, Mary Lamb's benevolent tap at my window-pane seldom failed to summon me out, and I was presently ensconced in a quiet corner of their sitting-room, half hid in some great man's shadow.

" Of the discourse of these *dii majores* I have no recollection now ; but the faces of some of them I can still partially recall. Hazlitt's face, for instance, keen and aggressive, with eyes that flashed out epigram ; Tom Hood's, a Methodist parson's face, not a ripple breaking the lines of it, though every word he dropped was a pun, and every pun roused roars of laughter; Leigh Hunt's, parcel genial, parcel democratic, with as much rabid politics on his lips as honey from Mount Hybla ; Miss Kelly [the little Barbara S. of 'Elia'], plain but engaging, the most unprofessional of actresses and unspoiled of women ; the bloom of the child on her cheek undefaced by the rouge, to speak in metaphors.

She was one of the most dearly welcome of Lamb's guests. Wordsworth's, farmerish and respectable, but with something of the great poet occasionally breaking out, and glorifying forehead and eyes." . . .

Mary did not escape her usual seizure. "You will understand my silence," writes Lamb to his Quaker friend, "when I tell you that my sister, on the very eve of entering into a new house we have taken at Enfield, was surprised with an attack of one of her sad, long illnesses, which deprive me of her society, though not of her domestication, for eight or nine weeks together. I see her, but it does her no good. But for this, we have the snuggest, most comfortable house, with everything most compact and desirable. Colebrook is a wilderness. The books, prints, etc., are come here, and the New River came down with us. The familiar prints, the busts, the Milton, seem scarce to have changed their rooms. One of her last observations was, 'How frightfully like this is to our room at Islington,' — our up-stair room she meant. We have tried quiet here for four months, and I will answer for the comfort of it enduring." And again, later: "I have scarce spirits to write. Nine weeks are completed, and Mary does not get any better. It is perfectly exhausting. Enfield and everything is very gloomy. But for long experience, I should fear her ever getting well."

She did get "pretty well and comfortable again" before the year was quite out, but it did not last long. Times grew sadder and sadder for the faithful brother. There are two long, oft-quoted letters to Bernard Barton, written in July, 1829, which who has ever read without a pang?

"My sister is again taken ill," he says, "and I am obliged to remove her out of the house for many weeks, I fear, before I can hope to have her again. I have been very desolate indeed. My loneliness is a little abated by our young friend Emma having just come here for her holidays, and a schoolfellow of hers that was with her. Still, the house is not the same, though she is the same. Mary had been pleasing herself with the prospect of seeing her at this time; and with all their company, the house feels at times a frightful solitude. . . . But town, with all my native hankering after it, is not what it was. . . . I was frightfully convinced of this as I passed houses and places — empty caskets now. I have ceased to care almost about anybody. The bodies I cared for are in graves or dispersed. . . . Less than a month I hope will bring home Mary. She is at Fulham,

looking better in her health than ever, but
sadly rambling, and scarce showing any pleasure in seeing me, or curiosity when I should
come again. But the old feelings will come
back again, and we shall drown old sorrows
over a game of piquet again. But 'tis a tedious
cut out of a life of fifty-four to lose twelve or
thirteen weeks every year or two. And to
make me more alone, our ill-tempered maid is
gone [Becky], who, with all her airs, was yet a
home-piece of furniture, a record of better
days. The young thing that has succeeded her
is good and attentive, but she is nothing; and
I have no one here to talk over old matters
with. Scolding and quarreling have something
of familiarity and a community of interest;
they imply acquaintance; they are of resent-
ment which is of the family of dearness.
Well, I shall write merrier anon. 'Tis the
present copy of my countenance I send, and to
complain is a little to alleviate. May you
enjoy yourself as far as the wicked world will
let you, and think that you are not quite alone,
as I am."

To the friends who came to see him he made
no complaints, nor showed a sad countenance;
but it was hard that he might not relieve his
drear solitude by the sights and sounds of
beloved London. "O never let the lying poets

be believed," he writes to Wordsworth, "who 'tice men from the cheerful haunts of streets; or think they mean it not of a country village. In the ruins of Palmyra I could gird myself up to solitude, or muse to the snorings of the Seven Sleepers; but to have a little teazing image of a town about one; country folks that do not look like country folks; shops two yards square; half a dozen apples and two penn'orth of over-looked gingerbread for the lofty fruit-erers of Oxford street; and for the immortal book and print stalls, a circulating library that stands still, where the show-picture is a last year's valentine. . . . The very blackguards here are degenerate; the topping gentry, stock-brokers; the passengers too many to insure your quiet or let you go about whistling or gaping, too few to be the fine, indifferent pageants of Fleet street. . . . A garden was the primitive prison till man, with Prome-thean felicity and boldness, luckily sinned himself out of it. Thence followed Babylon, Nineveh, Venice, London, haberdashers, gold-smiths, taverns, satires, epigrams, puns,— these all came in on the town part and the thither side of innocence." . . . In the same letter he announces that they have been obliged to give up home altogether, and have "taken a farewell of the pompous, troublesome trifle

called housekeeping, and settled down into
poor boarders and lodgers at next door with an
old couple, the Baucis and Baucida of dull
Enfield. Here we have nothing to do with our
victuals but to eat them, with the garden but
to see it grow, with the tax-gatherer but to
hear him knock, with the maid but to hear her
scolded. Scot and lot, butcher, baker, are
things unknown to us save as spectators of the
pageant. We are fed, we know not how;
quietists, confiding ravens. . . . Mary
must squeeze out a line *propria manu*, but
indeed her fingers have been incorrigibly nervous to letter-writing for a long interval.
'Twill please you all to hear that, though I fret
like a lion in a net, her present health and
spirits are better than they have been for some
time past. She is absolutely three years and
a half younger since we adopted this boarding
plan! . . . Under this roof I ought now
to take my rest, but that back-looking ambition,
more delightful, tells me I might yet be a
Londoner! Well, if ever we do move, we have
encumbrances the less to impede us; all our
furniture has faded under the auctioneer's
hammer, going for nothing, like the tarnished
frippery of the prodigal, and we have only a
spoon or two left to bless us. Clothed we came
into Enfield, and naked we must go out of it.
I would live in London shirtless, bookless."

Now that Mary was recovered they did venture to try once more the experiment of London lodgings at 24 Southampton Buildings, Holborn, where Hazlitt had often stayed. But the result was worse even than could have been anticipated. May 12, 1830, Lamb writes: "I have brought my sister to Enfield, being sure she had no hope of recovery in London. Her state of mind is deplorable beyond any example. I almost fear whether she has strength, at her time of life, ever to get out of it. Here she must be nursed and neither see nor hear of anything in the world out of her sick chamber. The mere hearing that Southey had called at our lodgings totally upset her. Pray see him or hear of him at Mr. Rickman's, and excuse my not writing to him. I dare not write or receive a letter in her presence."

Another old friend, the one whom, next to Coleridge, Wordsworth and Manning, Lamb valued most, died this year. Hazlitt's strength had been for some time declining; and during the summer of 1830 he lay at his lodgings, 6 Frith street, Soho, languishing in what was to prove his death-illness, though he was but fifty-two; his mind clear and active as ever, looking. back, as he said, upon his past life, which "seemed as if he had slept it out in a dream or shadow on the side of the hill of knowledge,

11

where he had fed on books, on thoughts, on pictures, and only heard in half murmurs the trampling of busy feet or the noises of the throng below." "I have had a happy life" were his last words. Unfortunate in love and marriage, perhaps scarcely capable of friendship, he found the warmth of life, the tie that bound him to humanity, in the fervor of his admiration for all that is great or beautiful or powerful in literature, in art, in heroic achievement. His ideas, as he said of himself, were "of so sinewy a character that they were in the nature of realities" to him. Lamb was by his death-bed that 18th of September.

Godwin still lived, but there seems to have been little intercourse between the old friends. Manning was often away travelling on the Continent. Martin Burney maintained his place "on the top scale of the Lambs' friendship ladder, on which an angel or two were still climbing, and some, alas! descending," and oftenest enlivening the solitude of Enfield. He "is as good and as odd as ever," writes Charles to Mrs. Hazlitt. "We had a dispute about the word 'heir,' which I contended was pronounced like 'air.' He said that might be in common parlance, or that we might so use it speaking of the 'Heir-at-Law,' a comedy, but that in the law courts it was necessary to give it a full aspiration and to say *hayer;* he thought it might even vitiate a cause if a counsel pronounced it otherwise. In conclusion he 'would consult Sergeant Wilde' — who gave it against him. Sometimes he falleth into the water; sometimes into the fire. He came down here and insisted on reading Virgil's *Eneid* all through with me (which he did), because a counsel must know Latin. Another time he read out all the Gospel of St. John, because Biblical quotations are very emphatic in a court of justice. A third time he would carve a fowl, which he did very illfavoredly, because 'we did not know how indispensable it was for a barrister to do all those things well. Those little things were of more consequence than we supposed.' So he goes on, harassing about the way to prosperity, and losing it; with a long head, but somewhat a wrong one — harum-scarum. Why does not his guardian angel look to him ? He deserves one; may be he has tired him out."

A cheerful glimpse of the brother and sister occurs now and then in the diary of their old friend, Crabb Robinson, in these days when the dark times were so long and the bright intervals so short and far between. March, 1832, he writes : "I walked to Enfield and found the Lambs in excellent state — not in high health, but, what is far better, quiet and cheerful. I had a very pleasant evening at whist. Lamb was very chatty and altogether as I could wish." And again in July: . . . "reached Lamb at the lucky moment before tea. After tea Lamb and I took a pleasant walk together. He was in excellent health and tolerable spirits, and was to-night quite eloquent in praise of Miss Isola. He says she is the most sensible girl and the best female talker he knows; . . . he is teaching her Italian without knowing the language himself." Two months later the same friend took Walter Savage Landor to pay them a visit. "We had scarcely an hour to chat with them, but it was enough to make Landor express himself delighted with the person of Mary Lamb and pleased with the conversation of Charles Lamb, though I thought him by no means at his ease, and Miss Lamb was quite silent."

Scarcely ever did Charles leave home for many hours together when Mary was there to brighten it; not even for the temptation of seeing the Wordsworths or Coleridge. "I want to see the Wordsworths," he writes, "but I do not much like to be all night away. It is dull enough to be here together, but it is duller to leave Mary; in short, it is painful;" and to Coleridge, who had been hurt by the long interval since he had seen them, Lamb writes:

" Not an unkind thought has passed in my brain about you ; but I have been wofully neglectful of you. . . . old loves to and hope of kind looks from the Gillmans when I come. If ever you thought an offense, much more wrote it against me, it must have been in the times of Noah, and the great waters swept it away. Mary's most kind love, and may be a wrong prophet of your bodings ! Here she is crying for mere love over your letter. I wring out less but not sincerer showers."

The spring of 1833 brought to Charles and Mary only the return of dark days. Lamb writes to Wordsworth : —

"Your letter, save in what respects your dear sister's health, cheered me in my new solitude. Mary is ill again. Her illnesses encroach yearly. The last was three months, followed by two of depression most dreadful. I look back upon her earlier attacks with longing: nice little durations of six weeks or so, followed by complete restoration, shocking as they were then to me. In short, half her life she is dead to me, and the other half is made anxious with fears and lookings forward to the next shock. With such prospects it seemed to me necessary that she should no longer live with me and be fluttered with continual removals; so I am come to live with her at a Mr. Walden's and his wife [at Edmonton], who take in patients, and have arranged to lodge and board us only. They have had the care of her before. I see little of her; alas! I too often hear her. *Sunt lachrymæ rerum!* and you and I must bear it.

"To lay a little more load on it, a circumstance has happened (*cujus pars magr_a fui*), and which at another crisis I should have more rejoiced in. I am about to lose my old and only walk companion, whose mirthful spirits were the 'youth of our house'—Emma Isola. I have her here now for a little while, but she is too nervous properly to be under such a roof, so she will make short visits—be no more an inmate. With my perfect approval and more than concurrence, she is to be wedded to Moxon at the end of August. So 'perish the roses and the flowers!'—how is it?

"Now to the brighter side. I am emancipated from the Westwoods, and I am with attentive people and younger. I am three or four miles nearer the great city; coaches half price less and going always, of which I will avail myself. I have few friends left there—one or two, though, most beloved. But London streets and faces cheer me inexpressibly, though not one known of the latter were remaining. . . . I am feeble but cheerful in this my genial hot weather. Walked sixteen miles yesterday. I can't read much in summer-time."

There was no sense of being "pulled up by the roots" now in these removals. Lamb had and could have no home, since she who had been its chief pride was in perpetual banishment from him and from herself. The following notelet which Talfourd, in his abundance, probably did not think worth publishing, at any rate shows, with mournful significance, how bitter were his recollections of Enfield, to which they had gone full of hope. It was written to Mr. Gillman's eldest son, a young clergyman, desirous of the incumbency of Enfield : —

"By a strange occurrence we have quitted Enfield *forever!* Oh! the happy eternity! Who is vicar or lecturer for that detestable place concerns us not. But Asbury, surgeon and a good fellow, has offered to get you a mover and seconder, and you may use my name freely to him. Except him and Dr. Creswell, I have no respectable acquaintance in the dreary village. At least my friends are all in the *public* line, and it might not suit to have it moved at a special vestry by John Gage at the Crown and Horseshoe, licensed victualler, and seconded by Joseph Horner of the Green Dragon, ditto, that the Rev. J. G. is a fit person to be lecturer, etc.

"My dear James, I wish you all success, but am too full of my own emancipation almost to congratulate any one else."

Miss Isola's wedding-day came, and still Mary's mind was under eclipse; but the announcement of the actual event restored her as by magic; and here is her own letter of congratulation to the bride and bridegroom — the last from her hand : —

"MY DEAR EMMA AND EDWARD MOXON : —

"Accept my sincere congratulations, and imagine more good wishes than my weak nerves will let me put into good, set words. The dreary blank of *unanswered questions* which I ventured to ask in vain was cleared up on the wedding-day by Mrs. W. taking a glass of wine, and, with a total change of countenance, begging leave to drink Mr. and Mrs. Moxon's health. It restored me from that moment, as if by an electric shock, to the entire possession of my senses. I never felt so calm and quiet after a similar illness as I do now. I feel as if all tears were wiped from my eyes and all care from my heart."

To which beautiful last words Charles adds :—

"DEARS AGAIN : — Your letter interrupted a seventeenth game at piquet which *we* were having after walking to Wright's and purchasing shoes We pass our time in cards, walks and reading. We attack Tasso soon. Never was such a calm or such a recovery. 'Tis her own words undictated."

Not Tasso only was attacked, but even Dante. "You will be amused to hear," he tells Carey, "that my sister and I have, with the aid of Emma, scrambled through the *Inferno* by the blessed furtherance of your polar-star translation. I think we scarce left anything unmade-out. But our partner has left us, and we have not yet resumed. Mary's chief pride in it was that she should some day brag of it to you."

The year 1834, the last of Lamb's life, opened gloomily. Early in February was written one of the saddest and sweetest of all his utterances concerning Mary. With the exception of a brief, mournful allusion to her in his latest letter to Wordsworth, these were his last written words about her, and they breathe the same tenderness and unswerving devotion at the close of his life-long struggle and endurance for her sake as those he wrote when it began. The letter is to Miss Fryer, an old schoolfellow of Emma Isola: "Your letter found me just returned from keeping my birthday (pretty innocent!) at Dover street [the Moxons]. I see them pretty often. In one word, be less uneasy about me; I bear my privations very well; I am not in the depths of desolation, as heretofore. Your admonitions are not lost upon me.

Your kindness has sunk into my heart. Have faith in me. It is no new thing for me to be left to my sister. When she is not violent her rambling chat is better to me than the sense and sanity of this world. Her heart is obscured, not buried; it breaks out occasionally, and one can discern a strong mind struggling with the billows that have gone over it. I could be nowhere happier than under the same roof with her. Her memory is unnaturally strong; and from ages past, if we may so call the earliest records of our poor life, she fetches thousands of names and things that never would have dawned upon me again, and thousands from the ten years she lived before me. What took place from early girlhood to her coming of age principally live again (every important thing and every trifle) in her brain, with the vividness of real presence. For twelve hours incessantly she will pour out, without intermission, all her past life, forgetting nothing, pouring out name after name to the Waldens, as a dream, sense and nonsense, truth and errors huddled together, a medley between inspiration and possession. What things we are! I know you will bear with me talking of things. It seems to ease me, for I have nobody to tell these things to now." . . .

A week later was written that last little

letter to Wordsworth [the reader will recognize
Louisa Martin — Monkey — so prettily described
in Lamb's first letter to Hazlitt]: "I write
from a house of mourning. The oldest and
best friends I have left are in trouble. A
branch of them (and they of the best stock of
God's creatures, I believe) is establishing a
school at Carlisle. Her name is Louisa Martin.
For thirty years she has been tried by me, and
on her behavior I would stake my soul. Oh!
if you could recommend her, how would I love
you — if I could love you better! Pray recommend her. She is as good a human creature —
next to my sister, perhaps, the most exemplary
female I ever knew. Moxon tells me you would
like a letter from me; you shall have one.
This I cannot mingle up with any nonsense
which you usually tolerate from C. Lamb.
Poor Mary is ill again, after a short, lucid interval of four or five months. In short, I may call
her half dead to me. Good you are to me.
Yours, with fervor of friendship, forever."

The dearest friend of all, Coleridge, long in
declining health — the "hooded eagle, flagging
wearily" — was lying this spring and summer
in his last painful illness; heart-disease chiefly,
but complicated with other sources of suffering,
borne with heroic patience. Thoughts of his
youth came to him, he said, "like breezes from

the Spice Islands;" and under the title of that poem written in the glorious Nether Stowey days when Charles was his guest — *This Lime-tree Bower my Prison* — he wrote a little while before he died : —

Charles and Mary Lamb,

Dear to my heart, yea, as it were *my heart*,

S. T. C. Æt. 63, 1834.

1797
1834
———
37 years!

He drew his last breath on the 25th of July. At first Lamb seemed wholly unable to grasp the fact that he was gone. "Coleridge is dead!" he murmured continually, as if to convince himself. He "grieved that he could not grieve." "But since," he wrote in that beautiful memorial of his friend, the last fragment shaped by his hand — "but since, I feel how great a part of me he was. His great and dear spirit haunts me. . . . He was my fifty-year-old friend without a dissension. Never saw I his likeness, nor probably the world can see it again. I seem to love the house he died at more passionately than when he lived. I love the faithful Gillmans more than while they exercised their virtues towards him living. What was his mansion is consecrated to me a chapel."

A month after this was written Charles Lamb
followed his friend. A seemingly slight accident, a fall which wounded his face, brought on
erysipelas, and he sank rapidly, dying the 27th
December, 1834. For once, Mary's affliction
befriended her. Though her mind was not
wholly obscured at the time, for she was able to
show the spot in Edmonton churchyard where
her brother had wished to be buried, yet it was
so far deadened that she was unable to comprehend what had befallen her; and thus she
remained for nearly a year.

None thought of Mary with tenderer sympathy than Landor, or strove with more sincerity
to offer "consolation to the finest genius that
ever descended on the heart of woman," as he
fervently described her. "When I first heard
of the loss that all his friends, and many that
never were his friends, sustained in him," he
wrote to Crabb Robinson, "no thought took
possession of my mind except the anguish of his
sister. That very night, before I closed my
eyes, I composed this : —

TO THE SISTER OF CHARLES LAMB.

Comfort thee, O thou mourner ! yet awhile
Again shall Elia's smile
Refresh thy heart, whose heart can ache no more.
What is it we deplore?

> He leaves behind him, freed from grief and years,
> Far worthier things than tears,
> The love of friends without a single foe;
> Unequalled lot below!
> His gentle soul, his genius, these are thine;
> Shalt thou for these repine?
> He may have left the lowly walks of men;
> Left them he has; what then?
> Are not his footsteps followed by the eyes
> Of all the good and wise?
> Though the warm day is over, yet they seek
> Upon the lofty peak
> Of his pure mind, the roseate light that glows
> O'er death's perennial snows.
> Behold him! From the spirits of the blest
> He speaks: he bids thee rest."

About a month after her brother's death, their faithful old friend, Crabb Robinson, went to see Mary. "She was neither violent nor unhappy," he wrote in his diary, "nor was she entirely without sense. She was, however, out of her mind, as the expression is, but she could combine ideas, though imperfectly. On my going into the room where she was sitting with Mr. Walden, she exclaimed, with great vivacity, 'Oh! here's *Crabby.*' She gave me her hand with great cordiality, and said, 'Now, this is very kind — not merely good-natured, but very, very kind to come and see me in my affliction.' And then she ran on about the unhappy, insane family of my old friend——. Her mind seemed to turn to subjects connected with insanity as well as to her brother's death. She spoke of Charles, of his birth, and said that he was a weakly but very pretty child."

In a year's time she was herself once more; calm, even cheerful; able, now and then, to meet old friends at the Moxons'. She refused to leave Edmonton. "*He* was there asleep in the old churchyard, beneath the turf near which they had stood together, and had selected for a resting-place: to this spot she used, when well, to stroll out mournfully in the evening, and to this spot she would contrive to lead any friend who came in summer evenings to drink tea, and went out with her afterwards for a walk." Out of very love she was content to be the one left alone; and found a truth in Wordsworth's beautiful saying, that "a grave is a tranquillizing object; resignation, in course of time, springs up from it as naturally as the wild flowers besprinkle the turf."

Lucid intervals continued, for a few years longer, to alternate with ever-lengthening periods of darkness. That mysterious brain was not even yet wholly wrecked by the eighty years of storms that had broken over it. Even when the mind seemed gone the heart kept some of its fine instincts. She learned to bear her solitude very patiently, and was gentle and

kind always. Towards 1840 her friends per-
suaded her to remove to Alpha Road, St. John's
Wood, that she might be nearer to them.
Thirteen years she survived her brother, and
then was laid in the same grave with him at
Edmonton, May 28th, 1847; a scanty remnant
of the old friends gathering round — "Martin
Burney refusing to be comforted."

Coleridge looked upon Lamb "as one hover-
ing between heaven and earth, neither hoping
much nor fearing anything." Or, as he himself
once, with infinite sweetness, put it, "Poor Elia
does not pretend to so very clear revelations of
a future state of being. He stumbles about
dark mountains at best; but he knows at least
how to be thankful for this life, and is too
thankful indeed for certain relationships lent
him here, not to tremble for a possible resump-
tion of the gift." Of Mary it may be said that
she hoped all things and feared nothing—
wisest, noblest attitude of the human soul
toward the Unknown.

FAMOUS WOMEN SERIES.

GEORGE SAND.

By BERTHA THOMAS.

One volume. 16mo. Cloth. Price, $1.00.

"Miss Thomas has accomplished a difficult task with as much good sense as good feeling. She presents the main facts of George Sand's life, extenuating nothing, and setting naught down in malice, but wisely leaving her readers to form their own conclusions. Everybody knows that it was not such a life as the women of England and America are accustomed to live, and as the worst of men are glad to have them live. . . . Whatever may be said against it, its result on George Sand was not what it would have been upon an English or American woman of genius." — *New York Mail and Express.*

"This is a volume of the 'Famous Women Series,' which was begun so well with George Eliot and Emily Brontë. The book is a review and critical analysis of George Sand's life and work, by no means a detailed biography. Amantine Lucile Aurore Dupin, the maiden, or Mme. Dudevant, the married woman, is forgotten in the renown of the pseudonym George Sand.

"Altogether, George Sand, with all her excesses and defects, is a representative woman, one of the names of the nineteenth century. She was great among the greatest, the friend and compeer of the finest intellects, and Miss Thomas's essay will be a useful and agreeable introduction to a more extended study of her life and works." — *Knickerbocker.*

"The biography of this famous woman, by Miss Thomas, is the only one in existence. Those who have awaited it with pleasurable anticipation, but with some trepidation as to the treatment of the erratic side of her character, cannot fail to be pleased with the skill by which it is done. It is the best production on George Sand that has yet been published. The author modestly refers to it as a sketch, which it undoubtedly is, but a sketch that gives a just and discriminating analysis of George Sand's life, tastes, occupations, and of the motives and impulses which prompted her unconventional actions, that were misunderstood by a narrow public. The difficulties encountered by the writer in describing this remarkable character are shown in the first line of the opening chapter, which says, 'In naming George Sand we name something more exceptional than even a great genius.' That tells the whole story. Misconstruction, condemnation, and isolation are the penalties enforced upon the great leaders in the realm of advanced thought, by the bigoted people of their time. The thinkers soar beyond the common herd, whose soul-wings are not strong enough to fly aloft to clearer atmospheres, and consequently they censure or ridicule what they are powerless to reach. George Sand, even to a greater extent than her contemporary, George Eliot, was a victim to ignorant social prejudices, but even the conservative world was forced to recognize the matchless genius of these two extraordinary women, each widely different in her character and method of thought and writing. . . . She has told much that is good which has been untold, and just what will interest the reader, and no more, in the same easy, entertaining style that characterizes all of these unpretentious biographies." — *Hartford Times.*

Sold everywhere. Mailed, post-paid, on receipt of price, by the publishers,

ROBERTS BROTHERS, Boston.

Famous Women Series.

GEORGE ELIOT.

By MATHILDE BLIND.

One vol. 16mo. Cloth. Price, $1.00.

"Messrs. Roberts Brothers begin a series of Biographies of Famous Women with a life of George Eliot, by Mathilde Blind. The idea of the series is an excellent one, and the reputation of its publishers is a guarantee for its adequate execution. This book contains about three hundred pages in open type, and not only collects and condenses the main facts that are known in regard to the history of George Eliot, but supplies other material from personal research. It is agreeably written, and with a good idea of proportion in a memoir of its size. The critical study of its subject's works, which is made in the order of their appearance, is particularly well done. In fact, good taste and good judgment pervade the memoir throughout." — *Saturday Evening Gazette.*

"Miss Blind's little book is written with admirable good taste and judgment, and with notable self-restraint. It does not weary the reader with critical discursiveness, nor with attempts to search out high-flown meanings and recondite oracles in the plain 'yea' and 'nay' of life. It is a graceful and unpretentious little biography, and tells all that need be told concerning one of the greatest writers of the time. It is a deeply interesting if not fascinating woman whom Miss Blind presents," says the New York *Tribune.*

"Miss Blind's little biographical study of George Eliot is written with sympathy and good taste, and is very welcome. It gives us a graphic if not elaborate sketch of the personality and development of the great novelist, is particularly full and authentic concerning her earlier years, tells enough of the leading motives in her work to give the general reader a lucid idea of the true drift and purpose of her art, and analyzes carefully her various writings, with no attempt at profound criticism or fine writing, but with appreciation, insight, and a clear grasp of those underlying psychological principles which are so closely interwoven in every production that came from her pen." — *Traveller.*

"The lives of few great writers have attracted more curiosity and speculation than that of George Eliot. Had she only lived earlier in the century she might easily have become the centre of a mythos. As it is, many of the anecdotes commonly repeated about her are made up largely of fable. It is therefore, well, before it is too late, to reduce the true story of her career to the lowest terms, and this service has been well done by the author of present volume." — *Philadelphia Press.*

Sold by all booksellers, or mailed, post-paid, on price, by the publishers,

ROBERTS BROTHE